REDEEMING TIME

REDEEMING TIME

the wisdom of ancient jewish and christian festal calendars

BRUCE CHILTON

© 2002 by Hendrickson Publishers, Inc.
P. O. Box 3473
Peabody, Massachusetts 01961–3473

Printed in the United States of America

First Printing — October 2002

Library of Congress Cataloging-in-Publication Data

Chilton, Bruce.
    Redeeming time : the wisdom of ancient Jewish and Christian festal calendars / Bruce Chilton.
        p. cm.
    Includes bibliographical references and index.
    ISBN 1-56563-380-6 (hardcover : alk. paper)
    1. Fasts and feasts in the Bible.   2. Time—Religious aspects—Christianity   I. Title.
    BS680.F37 C48 2002
    263—dc21
                                            2002006653

Contents

Preface

While engaged in completing the manuscript of this book, I stood in line for lunch inside Nashville's Opryland. Somehow, that was the site for the thousands of scholars who attended the 2000 conference of the Society of Biblical Literature and the American Academy of Religion.

A few people ahead, a former student introduced herself, one of the first I had taught when I returned to America from England in 1985. Full of the happy news of her recent appointment to teach, she became somewhat sheepish when she told me she had written her dissertation in theology, rather than New Testament. But since the New Testament itself is theological in intent and idiom, I said her news was all good as far as I was concerned.

She had every right to look bemused (and did). Typically, New Testament writings (and the Gospels in particular) have been treated as if they were not really theological, but rather a unique kind of history. Moving beyond that inhibiting model involves at least two sorts of analysis. One is to show that the Gospels do not trade in what we would call historical facts, although inferences may be drawn about Jesus and his movement from what they say. The other is to embed the Gospels intellectually in the theological issues they addressed and then handed on to the Christian theology they were crucial in producing.

The natural language of the first sort of analysis is an explanatory account of what we can infer about Jesus and his followers. The second is a more philosophical enterprise, aimed at linking the achievement of the Gospels to continuing questions concerning the realities that matter most, whether human or divine.

While developing an extended project of narrative inference, the editors at Henrickson asked me to work on the question of festal time in the New Testament. As a result of their confidence (and patience), I have been able to reflect in a philosophical idiom at the same time that I was concentrating on a narrative concerning Jesus.[1]

The result is not only a different piece of work, but work in a different genre. But that does not surprise me: one mark of a genuinely theological question is that it demands its own genre to be posed and addressed.

Lent 2001

---

[1] *Rabbi Jesus: An Intimate Biography* (New York: Doubleday, 2000).

CHAPTER ONE

Introduction: finding time

Learning from cultures which are not ours

Those of us living in any society which styles itself as "developed," who have been formed by the culture of the West, are inclined to take it for granted that our standards (as well as our problems) are global. We even speak of differences between the "developed world" and the "developing world." Our unspoken assumption is that we are where humanity should be, and that other societies are to be measured insofar as they approach us. We have made our society into a "world," and then we make that "world" (as "developed") into the aspiration of everyone on the planet. Enough people on the physical earth have accepted that aspiration to render this picture plausible, at least in military and economic terms.

It is an open question whether as many people would accept our doctrine of "development" without the effort of advertising that comes with it. But advertising is our expertise, both in our overt efforts and in our implicit recommendation of ourselves—often through officially global organizations—by means of the standards of economic, political, and social life which we endorse for the use of others.

When the construct of the "developed world" is imposed on the globe in spatial terms, it naturally makes what is not "developed" into the "developing world": then everyone overseas or on our borders is understood to be heading in the American direction. This geographical apartheid has troubled our language. The phrase "developing world" came into fashion during the 1960s, on the grounds that it was demeaning to refer to the "underdeveloped world."[1]

---

[1] A book published in 1965 illustrates the change in usage. The title refers to "developing nations," the foreword to "underdeveloped areas," and the

Those who have set themselves up as arbiters of politically correct language have for some reason been slow to point out that all human societies (including our own) are, by their cultural identity, already "developed"—at the same time they are "developing"—with regard to their own structures of what people are to do, how they are to feel, and the beliefs they take as true.

The received opinion of what "development" means has resulted in an apartheid of time no less distorting than the apartheid of geography. When the notion of the "developed world" is imposed on the globe by looking back in time in historical terms, it naturally results in turning what is not "developed" into the opposite of modern. The "early modern world," the "pre-modern world," and the "ancient world" are increasingly fashionable categories in academic writing and teaching.[2] As more and more histories and ethnographies are added to what is studied, those broad categories inevitably include more and more societies, but with ever less specificity. Anyone actually familiar with the particulars of how human thought and feeling and action have been construed in human experience within distinctive histories (each with a chronological logic all its own) will rightly complain about the odd kind of intellectual imperialism which makes "us" the standard of everything else. This imperialism has advanced to the point that "they" all begin to look alike in being back there in a "pre-modern" or "ancient" past, which is defined principally by not being the present.

A similar problem has beset the discussion of the term "primitive" among anthropologists.[3] In that case, there seems to be a better awareness than among historians that inquirers must be aware of

---

introduction to "economically underdeveloped areas of the world" (see Eloise G. ReQua and Jane Statham, *The Developing Nations: A Guide to Information Sources* [Management Information Guide 5; Detroit: Gale, 1965]). A map on the inside cover distinguishes "highly developed," "semi-developed," "under-developed," and "planned" economies. What is really mapped here, of course, is the ideological frontier of the Cold War.

[2] For an exercise in exploring such categories that is both thoughtful and playful, see John Docker, *Postmodernism and Popular Culture: A Cultural History* (Cambridge: Cambridge University Press, 1994). On p. 274 he defines the early modern period as between 1500 and 1800 in current usage. Formerly, that period would have been understood to include the Renaissance, the Reformation, and the Enlightenment. Those designations carry obvious limitations, but it is not evident that "early modern" is any less limited. A cautionary treatment of recent trends is available in Gertrude Himmelfarb, *The New History and the Old* (Cambridge, Mass.: Belknap, 1987).

[3] See Marianna Torgovnich, *Gone Primitive: Savage Intellects, Modern Lives* (Chicago: University of Chicago, 1990).

the extent to which they impose their own categories on what they study. But some anthropologists and other cultural historians have betrayed a superficial grasp of the difficulty: they speak of "small scale" (as distinct from "large scale"), or "traditional" (as distinct from "modern"), and think they have solved the problem by avoiding language of the "primitive." They do not observe that all such designations write the distinction between "developed" and "developing" back into the record. And what all this replacement-language obscures is that, when we deal with any class of phenomena, the term "primitive" permits us to speak of its initial stage. When that stage is the focus of inquiry, later developments and ramifications (however beneficial people may consider them) can actually inhibit understanding. Primitive Christianity, for example, appeared as a type of Judaism in its own time, unlike its appearance later.

This primitive Christianity was anything but "traditional" in its time, and not "small scale" in comparison with many religious groups in the Greco-Roman experience. But that Christianity, the Christianity of the New Testament, is the precedent for those which followed in much the same way that evolution can be traced in natural history and other forms of cultural history.[4]

When "we" in the "modern world" (or the "post-modern world") look back, all other societies begin to look alike. The effect is similar to when we look, not back, but across—at societies so different from our own they do not even compete with ours in economic or military terms. Academic discussion helps to encourage such a viewpoint, no doubt inadvertently, by speaking of "the other"[5] as any person or culture not identifiable with us, whether back in history or across a border.

---

[4] For that reason, I have maintained that "primitive Christianity" is a useful designation, and that the term "primitive" may be deployed in similar contexts; see Bruce Chilton, *The Temple of Jesus: His Sacrificial Program Within a Cultural History of Sacrifice* (University Park, Pa.: The Pennsylvania State University Press, 1992), 3–5, 23–4, 41, 114, 118–19, 137. See also *Judaism in the New Testament: Practices and Beliefs* (with Jacob Neusner; London and New York: Routledge, 1995); *Pure Kingdom: Jesus' Vision of God* (Studying the Historical Jesus 1; Grand Rapids: Eerdmans, 1996); *Trading Places: The Intersecting Histories of Judaism and Christianity* (with Jacob Neusner; Cleveland: Pilgrim, 1996); and *Christianity and Judaism—The Formative Categories* (with Jacob Neusner; 3 vols.; Harrisburg, Pa.: Trinity Press International, 1995–1997).

[5] What can be unfortunate about this habit is the tendency of reducing all "others" to that which is not like oneself. See Jean-Luc Nancy, "Sharing Voices," in *Transforming the Hermeneutic Context: From Nietzsche to Nancy* (Intersections: Philosophy and Critical Theory; Albany: State University of New York, 1990), 211–59.

These intellectual problems might be dismissed as being merely "academic" in a narrow sense. But the matter will appear profoundly and immediately ethical when we look at how we in the "world" that declares itself to be "developed" treat those in other societies, whether in different places or in different times. Just as there is an imperative of environmental ecology in the "developed" world, so there is an imperative of cultural ecology: we have so damaged other cultures—both "back" there in time, and "over" there in space—that we diminish our own awareness of human possibilities at the same time that we devastate genuine development among other people with the exportation of our least "developed" products. In that regard, any American living or traveling abroad can see that we put our most profitable foot, not our best foot, forward when we provide opportunities for "development."

Yet we can become aware, intellectually and ethically, of the problems posed by our own society's conduct. My own experience suggests that most people have given the matter some thought. A social scientist might well object that my experience is, by definition, "anecdotal." But that is in the nature of the case: experience is usually related by anecdote.

If we were to try to poll a large population with a view to seeing whether they had thought about how the "developed world" was an imposition on the cultures and peoples who actually live in the world, the result—enshrined in numbers—would be a reflection of how people related to interviewers at least as much as how they would relate their own experience. Unless an issue has already been raised within public awareness, it is not realistic to believe its importance can be tracked by polls.[6]

People who live in the "developed" or the "modern" or the "post-modern" world are presumably as selfish as any, but that does not in any way diminish their ability to be socially self-aware, to see that the society in which they live is narrow in its imagination and ethically ambivalent. When it comes to the question of time, in fact, most of us clearly recognize we have a problem.

The tempo bug: time as constraint

The widespread experience within our own culture is that time has become our greatest common constraint. Perhaps the clearest

---

[6] See Herbert F. Weisberg (with Jon A. Krosnick and Bruce D. Bowen), *An Introduction to Survey Research, Polling, and Data Analysis* (Thousand Oaks, Calif.: Sage, 1996).

recent indication of that was the persistent reporting of the "year 2000 bug" or "Y2K" (a secular apocalypticism which received greater attention than other forms of millennial fervor). January 1, 2000 came and went without the electronic apocalypse materializing, but also with no slackening of the Western preoccupation with time.

Where food, clothing, shelter, and medicine are in desperately short supply in the "developing world," the "developed world" has them all in abundance. Shortages (for example, in medical care for the poor) reflect problems of distribution more than failure in the production of what is needed. In the case of time, however, we feel ourselves generally impoverished. For that reason, the temporal character of our social existence should be a topic about which we are prepared to learn from cultures "back" there, "over" there.

An awareness of time's limitation is not likely, in and of itself, to lead very far. One might lack the leisure to pursue such thoughts. A lack of leisure is widely reported among people of my acquaintance. I have noticed, especially after I have been out of the country for some time, that when I ask people how they are, they are likely to answer, "Busy." They are unlikely to notice that they have not responded to my question.

Of course, being "busy" is not only a professional condition: the removal of leisure is a result not only of work but of the way in which family and entertainment and recreation and friends and personal hygiene and nutrition and home maintenance and civic responsibilities and worship have all been professionalized, each with what we have come increasingly to call an "industry." (That journalist's report on, say, the "entertainment industry," without observing that it is an oxymoron, will no doubt give future historians pause for thought and—let us hope—amusement.) The "industry" is ostensibly designed to "support" the activity, but its profit is made by making the activity into an occupation (or a preoccupation). With the business of such an "industry" comes not only the spending of money but the disposition of time. No one has enough time. Or so most people seem to think.

There is a deeper temporal paradox in a society constrained by time: people often feel they have time they do not know what to do with. When we are not too busy to be happy, or even to be aware of the degree of our happiness, time appears as something to be filled. Unfilled, time is a threat, and under that threat people commonly speak of being depressed.

Depression will usually be associated with particular causes for sadness—a relationship broken, a job lost, a loved one departed—but the mark of being depressed is that the object of one's grief fills any time given, and there is still time left over. Depression is the mirror image of busy-ness: "the sense that each moment is to be dreaded."[7] Depression may be triggered by events, and an influential study suggests that the process of becoming depressed takes between six months and a year.[8] That is what happens when, instead of time being pressed out with a multitude of cares, time becomes the threat of a single care constantly recurring. In its most acute forms, such depressions are manic; in more widely experienced forms, they show up as boredom.

But whether as mania or boredom, depression is as emblematic of the "modern," "post-modern," "developed" world as is its busyness and its business. Time is either scarce or vacant to a point that challenges endurance, and it is not rare to find people who complain that the constraints of time—both as too occupied and as too empty—are not endurable. A recent, courageous book by a sociologist about his own depression speaks of the twin burden of "frantic anxiety and a sense of grief": he reports time passing him by during the day and time at night filling his insomnia with dread.[9] From either pole of this problem of time, the fact of time as a *constraint* is a characteristic feature of the way we now live. This sense of constraint is immediate, often gripping and debilitating. Its power is not directly related to the ordinary awareness of people that one day they will die. The pressing issue of time has superseded even mortality as the persistent preoccupation of living when and where we do.

Time as constraint is a deeply felt, and often profoundly disturbing, feature of our lives, but time is also present to us under quite a different aspect.

Time as rhythm

At its most widely accessible and immediately enjoyable, this other aspect of time is experienced in music: in recurring, patterned ex-

---

[7] So Brett Silverstein and Deborah Perlick, *The Cost of Competence: Why Inequality Causes Depression, Eating Disorders, and Illness in Women* (New York: Oxford University Press, 1995), 46.

[8] See George W. Brown and Tirril Harris, *Social Origins of Depression: A Study of Psychiatric Disorder in Women* (New York: Free Press, 1978), 128.

[9] David A. Karp, *Speaking of Sadness: Depression, Disconnection, and the Meanings of Illness* (New York: Oxford University Press, 1996), 6.

pressions of rhythm and melody, and their interrelations.[10] But such patterns are also evident to us in the seasons of the year and the cycles of the sun, in the holidays we keep, in the phases of the moon, in the ebb and flow of tides (literally, in the ocean; figuratively, in the tidal movements of people to and from work or of birds in their waves of migration). Time in this sense is often called cyclical, in view of the importance of predictable recurrence in human experience.

But the recurrence that time brings is never simply repetition. In a musical composition, for example, one might "repeat" many units of the piece (of however many "bars"), but the fact that they are repeated at different moments within the piece as a whole gives them a distinctive quality to the hearer and the musician. Music shows us that, in human experience, literal repetition is impossible. One is always aware of events intervening between an act and its recurrence, so that what recurs—although it is recognizable—typically differs from what might have been expected. In our feelings as well as in our thoughts, whatever recurs happens in a new context and bears a new meaning.[11] As a recent theorist put the matter, musical time is "an encounter of two paradigms: that of memory, which increases as a musical piece moves toward its end, and that of expectation, which diminishes in the course of a composition."[12]

In music, and in every recurring pattern within human experience, this fact of the unrepeatability of exact recurrence is also inherent in a sense of time. Every autumn, every spring, the starlings which flock in the woods near my home may be said to repeat a pattern; that recurrence provides me with an experience which is both new and predictable on every occasion. Each time my experience is unique, and my reaction is different, although each time I mention to my family that the birds are there and we interrupt what we are doing to stand outside amidst thousands of chattering birds and

---

[10] See Malcom Budd, *Music and the Emotions: The Philosophical Theories* (London: Routledge, 1992), ix.

[11] But it is too easy to refer to context as creating meaning, because when an act recurs, it is automatically a part of the context involved. See Peter Kivy, *The Fine Art of Repetition: Essays in the Philosophy of Music* (Cambridge: Cambridge University Press, 1993), 327–59 (the essay's title is the same as the book's title).

[12] Eero Tarasti, *A Theory of Musical Semiotics* (Advances in Semiotics; Bloomington and Indianapolis: Indiana University Press, 1994), 289. A similar insight is pursued in Jay Rahn, *A Theory for All Music: Problems and Solutions in the Analysis of Non-Western Forms* (Toronto: University of Toronto Press, 1983).

dozens of confused squirrels, whose chant marks seasonal autumn or seasonal spring (whatever the calendar might say).

Part of what makes each event of recurrence unique, and therefore not a bare repetition, is that we are aware of the sequence of the pattern in relation to other events. That is true of a phrase of music and the arrival of the starlings, and in each case, too, we appreciate that there is to be an end of the sequence, as there was a beginning. Part of the pleasure of music involves just this sequencing.

Beginnings and endings are in life simply given to us, most palpably and incontrovertibly in the cases of birth and death. Music, dance, and drama (music's near relations)[13] provide us with a control over the intervals of experience in a way we almost never otherwise exercise. The free choice of intervals, including the beginning and the end, is precisely what we do not ordinarily enjoy during the course of our lives. The fact that this choice is exercised in musical, dance, and dramatic performance provides a dimension of pleasure: in the connection between performers and audience, the control of the intervals of experience seems to be shared. In good performance (as in good politics), there is no question of the will of a single person indulging its freedom by imposing it on everyone else.

The experience of time under the aspect of recurrence and interval, rather than under the constraining aspect of the over-commitment and emptiness of schedules, is what is usually talked about in philosophical and more generally academic discussion.[14] The dividing off of time's constraint from time's rhythm, however, is itself indicative of a typically modern dichotomy: in intellectual discourse we tend not to speak, not even to think, of that constraining time which almost eclipses the rhythmic time we would prefer to consider. That dichotomy is addressed, and potentially resolved, by a willingness to consider time more globally, as is done in the Judaic and Christian systems we are about to consult.

Dividing time, losing time

Yet the unproductive tendency among modern, academic thinkers to dichotomize time by no means ends where it concerns the

---

[13] So Aristotle's *Poetics* also includes painting (and poetry itself) among the mimetic arts. See Paul Woodruff, "Aristotle on Mimesis," in *Essays on Aristotle's Poetics* (ed. Amélie Oksenberg Rorty; Princeton: Princeton University, 1992), 73–95. "*Mimesis*" is also discussed below.

[14] See, for example, J. J. C. Smart, "Time," *The Encyclopedia of Philosophy* (ed. P. Edwards; New York: Macmillan and The Free Press, 1967), 8:126–34.

rhythm of time as contrasted with the constraint of time. Even within time's rhythm, where a more integrative perception appears to be a major strength of the experience, recurrence (usually called "cyclical time") is contrasted sharply with interval (usually called "linear" or historical time). It is commonplace to conceive of Greek thought as mythological and cyclical and of Hebrew thought as historical and linear.

In the period after World War II, just that division was radically questioned by Thorleif Boman,[15] an influential and perceptive Scandinavian scholar. In his view, Greek thought represented static thinking because it emphasized the rhythmic recurrence of events. Hebrew thought, by contrast, represented dynamic thinking, because it emphasized the uniqueness of events in their non-repeatable intervals. As he himself expresses the matter:

> For the Hebrews who have their existence in the temporal, the content of time plays the same rôle as the content of space plays for the Greeks. As the Greeks gave attention to the peculiarity of things, so the Hebrews minded the peculiarity of events. . . . *The Semitic concept of time is closely coincident with that of its contents* without which time would be quite impossible. The quantity of duration completely recedes behind the characteristic feature that enters with time or advances in it. Johannes Pedersen comes to the same conclusion when he distinguishes sharply between the Semitic understanding of time and ours. According to him, time is for us an abstraction since we distinguish time from the events that occur in time. The ancient Semites did not do this; for them time is determined by its content. Time is the notion of the occurrence; it is the stream of events.[16]

It should be stressed that Boman was not arguing for a simple opposition between cyclical thinking and linear thinking when it comes to time; indeed, it is part of the genuine strength of his consideration that recurrence *and* interval find their places within *both* the systems he engages.[17]

His point is rather that "the Greeks" (followed by "we Europeans"[18]) consider time to be exterior to events, while "the

---

[15] Thorleif Boman, *Hebrew Thought Compared with Greek* (trans. J. L. Moreau; The Library of History and Doctrine; Philadelphia: Westminster, 1960).

[16] Boman, *Hebrew Thought Compared with Greek*, 139.

[17] See Boman's entire chapter, "Time and Space," in *Hebrew Thought Compared with Greek*, 123–83.

[18] Boman, *Hebrew Thought Compared with Greek*, 138. On p. 149, "we" becomes "Indo-Germanic."

Hebrews" understand that time inheres within events. In his own way, he shows that time both as recurrence and as interval is recognized in any serious engagement with the question of time. Because events recur in his presentation of Greek thought, time as interval is incidental to them; because events are unique intervals in his presentation of Hebrew thought, time as recurrent is incidental to them.

The weak point of his analysis is his association of one emphasis essentially with one culture, and of the other emphasis essentially with the other culture. According to Boman, Greek culture's typical expression was myth, while Hebrew culture's was history, and especially salvation history. This analysis was built upon the category of salvation history, a conception widely current in international theology that had developed especially in Scandinavian thought. Its emphasis fell on how God intervenes in human history sequentially, in order to produce an understanding of salvation as a coherent account of the past. Salvation history *(Heilsgeschichte)* may be regarded as the Scandinavian wing of Neo-Orthodoxy, an attempt, especially fashionable after the Second World War, to read both the Bible and human experience in the light of the traditional, intellectual expressions of Christian faith.

Neo-Orthodoxy had its beginnings in the work of Karl Barth; Dietrich Bonhoeffer and Rudolf Bultmann were among its ablest defenders. All of them were prominent throughout their careers prior to the War, but post-War theology (particularly American theology)—in its attempt to find an international orientation that would serve as a biblically oriented model of human suffering and the hope of redemption—made salvation history into a principle of ecumenical discussion. Barth, Bonhoeffer, and Bultmann became standard points of reference in academic theology in the United States, and the influence of their work on the curricula of theological seminaries would be difficult to overestimate.[19]

Within the perspective of Neo-Orthodoxy, the reading of salvation history into the Bible is sensible. This interpretation follows the perspective of Augustine, the founder of global history in Christianity. Prior to Augustine, there was no coherent argument to the effect that human events were both consequential in their revelation of God and meaningfully sequential in their

---

[19] By way of example, see Sydney E. Ahlstrom, ed., *Theology in America: The Major Protestant Voices from Puritanism to Neo-Orthodoxy* (The American Heritage Series; Indianapolis: Bobbs-Merrill, 1967).

unfolding.[20] Those are the *sine qua non* of salvation history: divine meaning must attach to specific events and to the relationship among events for history to be redemptive. The assumption of Neo-Orthodoxy was that history was the category of all humanity's redemption and that anyone could see this progressive possibility. When Boman uses the "Hebrew mode of expression" to call on his readers "to stop thinking of time as something spatial, statically definable, almost visible, and instead appreciate time as the transcendental design of history, human as well as cosmic,"[21] this is transparently a theological argument. Since Neo-Orthodoxy was then regnant in mainline Protestant seminaries, such arguments were profoundly attractive.

But Boman wrote his book not as a theological piece but as an account of Greek and Hebrew *linguistics,* especially the verbal system in each language. That set him up for a trenchant and searching attack from James Barr, who was able rather easily to show that both Greek and Hebrew could express time as "cyclical" and time as "linear."[22] Barr's own vehemence by no means derived from philological and linguistic considerations alone. He was at a stage in his intellectual development in which he was preparing to take on the entire topic of Fundamentalism, on which he lectured for several years before and after he wrote a book with that title.[23]

Barr's *The Semantics of Biblical Language* and *Fundamentalism,* taken together, mark an important shift in the theological ground of American and British discussion. The salvation-historical foundation of theology, which had become axiomatic in the post-War period, was not only under attack: it was besieged, and retreat was about to be sounded. Although Barr's *Fundamentalism* claimed to be aimed at an extreme form of Christian faith, Barr in fact made no specific use of the "Fundamentals" which the viewpoint itself

---

[20] See Jacob Neusner and Bruce Chilton, *The Intellectual Foundations of Christian and Jewish Discourse: The Philosophy of Religious Argument* (London: Routledge, 1997), 154–67.

[21] Boman, *Hebrew Thought Compared with Greek,* 149.

[22] See *The Semantics of Biblical Language* (London: Oxford University Press, 1961), 46–88. Barr acknowledges that Boman is more critical than "the biblical theology school," and yet contends "that in his analysis of Hebrew and in his methods of using linguistic evidence Boman follows the same lines of those biblical theologians who have used linguistic evidence from Hebrew" (pp. 46–47). This is one of the reasons I view Boman as representative of Neo-Orthodoxy.

[23] See James Barr, *Fundamentalism* (Philadelphia: Westminster, 1977).

claims. Instead, Barr was attacking all literalistic attachments to salvation history under the rubric of "Fundamentalism."[24] This confusion of categories, between Fundamentalism and literalistic history, is frequently encountered in academic circles, and it is worth a moment's consideration to clarify the issue.

Fundamentalism

The Institute of Advanced Theology at Bard College hosted a conference called "Judeo-Christian Relations for a New Millennium."[25] Andrew Greeley, William Scott Green, and Jacob Neusner joined me in the conference. They made the occasion unusually interesting, but we also dovetailed the conference with a course at the College, so that seventeen students participated fully, as programmed contributors who gave presentations. This made for a unique experience for everyone who took part.

During my discussions with my students prior to this conference, they asked me to define "Fundamentalism" for them. I explained its five main tenets, held to be "essential and necessary" teachings by the Presbyterian General Assembly in 1910:[26] the accuracy of the Bible in its reflection of God (biblical "inerrancy"), the virgin birth of Jesus, his actual miracles, his atonement offered to God by shedding his blood, and his resurrection in the same body in which he died. The response of my students was direct and to the point: "But isn't that what all Christians believe?"

Their reaction was telling. It reflects how little impact academic theology over the past two hundred years has had on popular awareness in the United States. This academic theology understands Christianity as something far more symbolic and collective than the Fundamentalist insistence on the literal belief of the individual. My students' reaction confirms what survey after survey has

---

[24] Barr himself problematizes reference to literalism as a working definition of Fundamentalism (p. 1), but then he argues that actual reference to the "Fundamentals" is "not very important for the usage of its (sc. Fundamentalism's) usage in the present day" (p. 2). By the end of his book, however, by which point he promises a definition (p. 2), Barr stresses the tenet of inerrancy as the center of Fundamentalism (pp. 338–44).

[25] See *Forging a Common Future: Catholic, Judaic, and Protestant Relations for a New Millennium* (with Andrew M. Greeley, William Scott Green, and Jacob Neusner; Cleveland: Pilgrim, 1997).

[26] See Sydney E. Ahlstrom, *A Religious History of the American People* (New Haven: Yale University Press, 1973), 812–16.

suggested,[27] that the take on Christianity in the United States is along Fundamentalist lines.

Fundamentals came to be asserted in both Protestantism and Catholicism in response to two basic challenges. Both of those challenges were voiced during the nineteenth century and continue to be influential today.

The first challenge is best appreciated by considering the example of David Friedrich Strauss, whose first major work, *The Life of Jesus*, was published in 1835. It was so controversial that it was immediately assured many printings in several languages, but its publication also meant that Strauss would be denied teaching positions in Germany and Switzerland. Strauss, under the influence of the philosophy of Hegel, believed that Jesus in the Gospels embodies the synthesis between divinity and humanity, so that the texts should be read as symbols, not as literal history. The idea that the Gospels are symbolic has continued to exert a powerful influence, both among those who are sympathetic and among those who react against it.

The second major challenge was Darwin's *On the Origin of Species* (1859). The idea of evolution has since been applied in many difference domains, including the study of religion. In the development of theology, it leads to the assertion that we in the present are in a better position to understand the significance of past events— including the life of Jesus—than those who were alive at the time. Taken together with the reading of the Gospels as symbols, the principle of evolution makes for a strong tendency to reinterpret the Scriptures.

Among both Catholics and Protestants, the reaction against these two principles was to insist upon certain fundamentals as literally true. In 1870, the First Vatican Council promulgated the doctrine of papal infallibility. Among Protestants, the very name of Fundamentalism was embraced, in order to insist that the Scriptures themselves set the infallible standard of faith.

Through the nineteenth century and the first half of the twentieth century, resistance to the teaching of literal fundamentals was adamantly maintained among Catholics and Protestants. In France and England, those who used historical tools to assert a symbolic

---

[27] A recent article found an increase of commitment to the belief that "the Bible is the actual word of God," from 32% to 39% of respondents between 1994 and 1995; see John Williams, "More in Survey Say Religion a Big Part of Their Lives," *Houston Chronicle*, January 4, 1996.

and evolutionary approach to interpretation were called Modern-
ists. The most famous of them was Alfred Loisy, a French priest
who found it perfectly natural to deny the infallibility of any
human being, who doubted the virgin birth of Jesus, saw Jesus' miracles as symbols, did not believe God needed a payment in blood in
order to love us, and overtly denied resurrection in the same body.
For him, the meaning of the Gospels resided in their capacity to
transform the nature of our collective existence.[28]

The Protestant Walter Rauschenbusch espoused a similarly collective, but less academic, theology in New York City. He called his
message "the social gospel," and by it he intended to insist that the
purpose of the Gospels was to overturn the structures of capitalism
and to change totally the nature of our social life in the interests
of justice.[29]

These theologians were both praised and attacked for their symbolic, evolutionary brands of Christianity. The Vatican banned
Loisy's books; he himself submitted to their banning, and agreed
not to engage in publication. But he refused to say that his opinions
were wrong, and was excommunicated from the Catholic Church
by Pope Pius X in 1908. His isolation from the Church provided
him with a new opportunity: a position in the Collège de France.
Rauschenbusch was a Baptist pastor in Brooklyn during the final
years of the century, just as Fundamentalism was making itself felt;
he found a warmer welcome at the Rochester Theological Semi-
nary, where he taught from 1897. His claim that Christianity was
a matter of programmatic social action, rather than individual belief, found more support among intellectuals than in the Baptist
hierarchy.

Both these thinkers are influential today. Loisy's methods and
his claims (for example) that Moses did not write the Pentateuch
and that the Apostle John did not author the Gospel named after
him are now taught as standard in Catholic and Protestant seminaries. Similarly, part of the formation of any pastor—Protestant,
Catholic, or (come to that) Jewish—will routinely include training
in what most people would call social work and what Rauschenbusch saw as part of the gospel: counseling, community organizing,
mediation, and the like. In religious academies, Loisy and Rauschenbusch prevailed a long time ago.

---

[28] See Raymond de Boyer de Sainte Suzanne, *Alfred Loisy, entre la foi de
l'incroyance* (Paris: Centurion, 1968).
[29] See D. R. Sharpe, *Walter Rauschenbusch* (New York: Macmillan, 1942).

But the popular scene has evidenced a reaction against symbol and evolution as providing keys to assessing the Gospels. Overtly Fundamentalist forms of Protestantism and papalist[30] forms of Catholicism have enjoyed enormous growth in the United States since World War II. That is one reason for which those interested in religion in America have little choice but to deal with the claim of literal fundamentals in Christianity. Americans appear to want definitive answers, fairly easily assimilated, and either claim of infallibility—for the pope or for the Bible—seems to suit that need. Fundamentalisms, by the way, are not limited to the right. A noted feminist scholar recently informed me that only a woman could represent an inclusive understanding of gender at the conference I mentioned. That is an example of what I might call sexual fundamentalism.

The symbolic and evolutionary approach of Loisy and Rauschenbusch has nonetheless persisted. It has prospered better in Europe than in America, even in popular culture. Catholic Europe has largely made its peace with papal infallibility by restricting its validity to symbolic truth. (That explains, for example, why France is an international leader in the field of birth control.) Insofar as Protestantism is Fundamentalist at all there, it is largely as a result of American influence, especially by cable television. Because American academics still tend to look to Europe as an example, it is perhaps not surprising that our academies (including our seminaries) espouse a theology which is rarely spoken to the public at large, but which would be at home in Europe.

From that European perspective, it is a fairly easy step to confusing Fundamentalism with a devotion to literal history. From the vantage point of an emphasis upon symbol and evolution, the assertion of basic categories of revelation looks remarkably like an unsophisticated literalism. But Fundamentalism and literalism are in fact quite different. Barr's confusion of the two heralded a denial of history itself as a serviceable approach to the study of theology.[31]

---

[30] For the use of this term to signal a disproportionate devotion to the papacy, see Garry Wills, "The Vatican Monarchy," *New York Review of Books* 45.3 (February 1998): 20–25. In an earlier, less probing piece (which might be described as an assault *ad hominem*), Wills makes the connection between the papalism of John Paul II and Fundamentalism: "The Tragic Pope?" *New York Review of Books* 41.2 (December 1994): 4–7. Cf. Garry Wills, *Papal Sin: Structures of Deceit* (New York: Doubleday, 2000).

[31] I would suppose that much of this outcome was unintended, but his work is such a superb example of the theology of his time we may use it to track formative developments.

In that denial, academics found themselves in a strange alliance with the very Fundamentalists they enjoyed condemning.

The denial of history

By conflating a salvation-historical perspective with Fundamentalism, Barr joined and encouraged a theological change, away from the axiom that the time marked out in the Bible is linear, and for that reason expressive of a particular sequence of consequential events. Of course, what was really rejected was a view associated with Augustine,[32] not the Bible. But it was important for Barr to achieve that rejection in the fields of both linguistic discussion (by means of his assault on Boman) and interpretation (by means of his attack on "Fundamentalism"). The Bible, he showed, is not the property of salvation history. Or, in the language of our interest here: the Bible is not the property of progressive time, a neat sequence from beginning, through the middle, and to the end, which wraps the whole of human experience within a coherent package.

But then, Fundamentalists were also in the process of denying that salvation is subject to human history in a way much more vehement and emphatic than Barr's. They hold that the Fundamentals of faith are not contingent matters which history can confirm or deny, but absolute truths, axioms attested by the inspired Bible. The irony is that Barr and others of the liberal viewpoint he represented seemingly did not notice that they had joined with Fundamentalists in an assault on the primacy of history within theological discussion.[33]

Barr's blind spot in this regard is revealing. By confusing Fundamentalism with historicism, he did not observe that Fundamentalists are less committed to any particulars of history than they are to the theological account which is defined by what they themselves call Fundamentals. In aggregate, those Fundamentals assert that God

---

[32] In fact, Augustine was not as committed to the notion of progress as the movement of biblical theology in our period has been. Indeed, part of his purpose was to cope with the reality of evident evil in the world in the period after Christ. *The City of God* was occasioned, after all, by Alaric's sack of Rome in 410 C.E. See Chilton and Neusner, *Trading Places*, 167–209.

[33] Moreover, for all that Barr attacked the biblical theology movement, his own commitment has been to a biblical theology; see D. A. Knight, "Barr, James," *Dictionary of Biblical Interpretation* (ed. J. H. Hayes; Nashville: Abingdon, 1999), 98–99.

by miraculous means of atonement is reclaiming and therefore trans-figuring human nature in its flesh, and the Bible is read, not literally, but as the coherent witness to that absolute truth. Barr, by contrast, is committed in theological terms, not to precise linguistics or pris-tine history, but to his conception that the act of interpretation itself is redeeming for the interpreter. That is, both conservative Fundamentalists and the liberal Barr illustrate the retreat from sal-vation history which has been characteristic of American and Brit-ish theology since 1960.[34]

The details of the argument concerning linguistics and interpre-tation do not concern us here, but the retreat from the concept of the overarching significance of progressive time *is* of immediate import. What was going on in theological discussion was mirrored in wider intellectual trends, and also in political developments.

In theology, Fundamentalism squared off against Liberal inter-pretation, each of them ideologically committed and increasingly ahistorical in their basic orientation. And in literary discussion, structuralism and deconstruction vied for influence. Structuralism posited that in the development of language and literature, certain essentials of discourse could be discerned, and that without such dis-cernment, interpretation was impossible.[35] Deconstruction, in con-trast, insisted that meaning only occurs in the mind of the interpreter, by means of engagement with the text (and sometimes without that benefit, in theoretical discussions which non-Deconstructionists often find difficult or impossible to follow).[36]

The politics of this period, the final ideological push of the Cold War, saw the emergence in America and (to a lesser extent) in Europe of a Conservative agenda which, for the first time in the history of Conservatism, wedded itself first of all to economic prin-ciples (capital markets protected and extended by a strong military establishment, low-tax monetarism, no deficit in government, re-jection of the redistribution of wealth).[37] Several of these commit-ments (which approach to being fundamentals in some circles) were woven into the aspirations of Conservatives during the course

---

[34] In *The Anchor Bible Dictionary* (ed. D. N. Freedman; 6 vols.; New York: Doubleday, 1992), see John C. O'Neill, "Biblical Criticism," 1:725–30, and William Baird, "New Testament Criticism," 1:730–36.

[35] See Daniel Patte, *What is Structural Exegesis?* (Guides to Biblical Scholar-ship; Philadelphia: Fortress, 1976).

[36] See Christopher Norris, *Deconstruction, Theory and Practice* (New Accents; London: Routledge, 1991).

[37] See Ted Honderich, *Conservatism* (Boulder: Westview, 1991).

of the nineteenth and twentieth centuries, but this common, international program—from Reagan's America through Thatcher's Britain and on to Kohl's Germany and beyond—marks a stunning intellectual or ideological development in the global political and economic scene during the past fifty years. Of course, there are Conservatives who stand for more than market capitalism, just as there are Fundamentalists who stand for more than scriptural infallibility, but what is similar in both groups is agreement by consensus to a limited range of principles and objectives.

But the apparent triumph of Conservatism on "the right" is no more momentous than the equally startling implosion of Liberalism on "the left." American political discourse has even seen a move away from using the "L-word," as if it held the place of the term Communism a generation ago.[38] But the absence of agreed terminology among Liberals is not only the result of the successful challenge from the right. Liberals themselves, compared with the great advances before, during, and after World War II—by the Democratic Party in America, the Labour Party in England, the Socialists in France, and the Social Democrats in Germany—have lost at least as much specificity in program as the Conservatives have gained. That is a consequence not simply of factionalism (of which there is plenty, on left and right) but of a pronounced Liberal proclivity to put principle after personal inclination, program after personal preference. This helps to explain the uncertainty of much Liberal policy subsequent to victory in elections. As Deconstruction marks the victory of the interpreter over the text, so Liberalism has come to stand for the ascendancy of personal proclivity over conceptual platform.

So not only in theology, but also in the more general discussion of meaning, as well as in politics, we find ourselves divided between a programmatic attachment to fundamentals on the one hand, and a programmatic attachment to individual propensity on the other hand. The opposition of the two stances within each field of conflict is impossible to resolve, and what passes for discourse for that reason is shrill when the opposing stances meet, and self-referential when they do not. What is widely decried, from right and left, as a loss of civility in public discourse (both intellectual and political) is in fact even more corrosive than a simple lack of manners.

---

[38] Within a single year, two books appeared with the title, *Liberalism and Its Discontents,* one by Neal Patrick (Basingstoke: Macmillan, 1997), and the other by Alan Brinkley (Cambridge: Harvard University Press, 1998).

In the struggle between fundamentals and propensities, there are no rules of engagement. So the right can attack any target on the left for lacking one of the fundamental elements of civilization: the behavior and character of liberals can be used against them in public discussion. And the left can counter that all such allegations from the right are projections of self-interest, and deny that any propensities should be subject to such hindrance. Recently, journalists on both sides of the Atlantic told us more than we ever wanted to know about President Clinton, a sometime intern in the White House, and Kenneth Starr. The posturing on both sides, the lurid reporting in virtually all public media, and the factional confusion of the United States Congress are perhaps the only instructive parts of that story. The Independent Counsel managed to extend his brief from investigating a land fraud to asking a private citizen and her mother about conversations they had about sexual encounters. The President and his advisers, in a skilled deployment of the hermeneutics of the left, pursued the pursuers by turning discussion to the motivations and interests of the Independent Counsel and his team. A better parable (or caricature) for the state of public discussion in the United States could not have been invented.

The most obvious victim of the charade was the intern herself, who after all made no public or legal complaint. Her sexual history became an issue when a friend tape-recorded a conversation which she relayed to the Independent Counsel, and the reaction of the White House was to impugn the reliability of what the intern might say. This invasion of her privacy was defended in much commentary by the probability she would write a book about her ordeal, which she in fact did. So the victim was not a victim, because she eventually profited from the theft of her privacy. Privacy itself, the right to be secure in one's person,[39] is defended neither by "Conservatives," who suffer from amnesia in regard to that Constitutional fundamental, nor by "Liberals," who have kept repeating since the 1960s that "the personal is political," without explaining what they might mean by that.

How can the sense of crucial distinctions in discourse—between private and public, between invective and argument, between programmatic agenda and analysis—have been eroded so quickly and seemingly permanently? With the close of the Cold War, Francis

---

[39] The fourth amendment to the Constitution states, "The right of the people to be secure in their persons, houses, papers, and effects, against unreasonable searches and seizures, shall not be violated. . . ."

Fukuyama wrote a controversial article, and then a book, called *The End of History*. He argued that history in the modern understanding is driven by conflict among nation-states; historians measure the importance of events by the influence of those events on the story of national contentions. Once such contentions come to an end, so does history.[40] The thesis was easily picked apart, since the emergence of the United States as the only remaining state with genuinely global power was never likely to bring more stability to international relations than the confrontation of the two "Super Powers" had ensured. Events since the publication of his work have only underscored that: the ideological freeze of two single ideas at loggerheads during the Cold War has melted down not to the dominance of a single, surviving idea, but to a multiplicity of new contenders for consideration.

But Fukuyama has been telling us something profoundly important about the way we in the West have sought to deal with the new situation. (He has, in his own way, shown us in politics what James Barr showed us in theology.) We have, on the right and on the left, disinvented history. On the right, alleged fundamentals of market capitalism are constantly invoked, which were discredited during the nineteenth century. Only willful ignorance can forget the child labor, the black lung disease among miners, the inhuman conditions imposed on seamstresses, which only legislation (and certainly not the "free" market) ended and which today are virtually unknown in the United States, even as Americans tolerate them in other countries that we trade with. On the left, the very history which might have been used to make a cogent case against such abuses has been dissolved into a series of allegedly multicultural vignettes, whose apparent moral is that all sorts of behavior can be legitimated. So William Bennett can say only he is really right, because his principles are correct,[41] and Cornell West can say only he is really correct, because his heart is in the right place.[42]

---

[40] See Francis Fukuyama, *The End of History and the Last Man* (New York: Avon, 1993).

[41] See William J. Bennett, *The Death of Outrage: Bill Clinton and the Assault on American Ideals* (New York: Macmillan, 1999).

[42] See Cornell West, *Roots of Violence* (New York: Basic, 1997).

CHAPTER TWO

Wisdoms of time in ancient calendars

Time's rhythm and constraints

History has ended, then, only in the sense that everything is happening at just the moment when we are having trouble explaining events, because we believe we are locked into two opposing approaches, favoring either programmatic fundamentals or personal propensities. My purpose here is not to announce that there is some third way, because at this stage that would seem to be a glib response. (That such a way will emerge seems to me a reasonable hope, because the diagnosis of our dilemma is possible. Nonetheless, the contradiction between fundamentals and propensities is not easily resolved.) But we can, in two steps, see that our typically modern (or post-modern) dilemma—how to speak across the cavern of fundamentals and propensities—may in fact be addressed by means of the wisdom of ancient cultures.

The first step is to understand that we have lost a historical sense. Reference has already been made to why that loss has occurred; that it has happened is widely agreed. The second step builds on our distinction between time as constraint and time as rhythm. The constraint of time is more and more apparent in the character of our common and our private lives (especially now that the distinction between the public and the private has been eroded). But the rhythm of time is a totally different matter: recurrence and interval are precisely what history investigates and rejoices in. And the insight that time's rhythm is woven into our lives, that recurrence and interval are not only personal experiences but inherently human realities, is lost when history is ended. The eclipse of history and the loss of time's rhythm are directly related to one another.

Values have also become difficult to discuss as we have lost a productive sense of time. Values are either pressed out of overly full schedules or they are overwhelmed in the despair that time is an open chasm.

So the sense of growing constraint and decreasing rhythm, the feeling that time crushes us more than it articulates and develops who we are, is more than anecdotal. The complaints that we are too busy, the complaints that we are too depressed, are too persistent to be discounted as random or unimportant. And now we can see that they are to be associated with the complaint both that public life has become unacceptably crude and that private life has been invaded by public life. Robert Hughes[1] has spoken of a "culture of complaint," and his observation of how it has become fashionable to portray oneself as a victim is incisive. But he by no means denies that the complaints are there; he wishes only to show—and show he does—that further complaint is no answer to the problem.

How to proceed? Both Judaism and Christianity accessibly provide—within their sacred Scriptures—calendars and explanations of time's rhythm. Moreover, each provides accounts of how the rhythm of festal joy, practiced and understood, stands in relation to the intervals of time that are collected in communal memories that are cherished within these comprehensive religious systems. The fact that it is now widely admitted that "Hebrew" thinking is not purely "linear," any more than "Greek" thinking is purely "cyclical," does not mean the sense of time within Judaism and Christianity are uninstructive. As a matter of fact, the relationship between time's rhythm and time's interval is exactly what we need to be instructed in, and that is precisely what the Scriptures can teach us.

Our inquiry, then, is to be academic in the sense that we wish to understand festal time critically, but it is not academic in the sense that it is removed from the substance of our experience as human beings. Here we wish to learn from what we can understand of the scriptural calendars of Judaism and Christianity. In that endeavor, I have benefited a great deal from a particular group of investigators, all of them influenced by the work of Austin Farrer[2] and Philip

---

[1] See Robert Hughes, *Culture of Complaint: The Fraying of America* (New York: Oxford University Press, 1993).

[2] See Michael D. Goulder, "Farrer, Austin Marsden (1904–1968)," *Dictionary of Biblical Interpretation* (ed. J. H. Hayes; Nashville: Abingdon, 1999), 387–88.

Carrington[3] during the 1950s. Farrer and Carrington independently hit upon the idea of explaining the growth of the New Testament on the basis of lectionary readings—the Scriptures recited at particular times within the liturgical life of Israel. Farrer concentrated on the Revelation, and Carrington on Mark. Then Aileen Guilding, a student of Farrer's, pursued this line of study in John's Gospel,[4] and (most influentially) Michael Goulder carried on in respect to Matthew and Mark, and then returned to Luke in particular.[5] Goulder's work has recently found an intelligent and effective popularizer in the shape of John Shelby Spong[6] in the United States.

All of this work has been interesting and detailed (sometimes to the point of causing bewilderment), but in one respect it has been even easier to attack than Boman's suggestion about time. The simple fact is that the lectionaries of Judaism which are attested in rabbinic literature are much later than the New Testament, and there is no reason to suppose that any fully worked-out system was widely available during the first century. Leon Morris[7] brought that stubborn fact to bear on Guilding's elaborate reconstruction of precise readings, and Morris's criticism has also been applied to the others named here.

So while I have learned from the work of Farrer and Carrington and their entourage, I have also consciously developed a distinct line of approach. I do not assume we can know what precise readings were used in the first century, nor that Christians were in the habit of simply repeating in their worship those passages of Scripture they may have heard in synagogues. Yet when a given feast of Judaism and Christianity associates itself with a motif of Scripture, any reader would have to be obtuse not to recognize that fact. The link between Passover and the exodus from Egypt, for example,

---

[3] Philip Carrington, *The Primitive Christian Calendar* (Cambridge: Cambridge University Press, 1952), and *According to Mark* (Cambridge: Cambridge University Press, 1960).

[4] Aileen Guilding, *The Fourth Gospel and Jewish Worship* (Oxford: Clarendon, 1960).

[5] See Michael D. Goulder, *Midrash and Lection in Matthew* (London: SPCK, 1974); *The Evangelists' Calendar* (London: SPCK, 1978); *Luke: A New Paradigm* (Journal for the Study of the New Testament: Supplement Series 20; Sheffield: JSOT, 1989).

[6] John Shelby Spong, *Liberating the Gospels: Reading the Bible with Jewish Eyes* (San Francisco: HarperSanFrancisco, 1996).

[7] Leon Morris, *The New Testament and the Jewish Lectionaries* (London: Tyndale, 1964).

does not require a complex theory of what exact readings from the Torah, tied to what exact reading from the Prophets, were in use in the first century. The fallacy of the approach pioneered by Farrer and Carrington is precisely that it presses what we *do* know—that Judaism and Christianity were festal religions in relation to one another, both of which celebrated time's rhythm and time's interval, into what we can*not* know—what precise lectionaries were followed. But our inability to specify lectionaries by no means erases the formative influence of religious festivals on Judaism and Christianity.

The tendency of scholarship to reduce the festal calendar to what lectionary was followed is yet another illustration of how an impaired grasp of time inhibits intellectual work. Farrer and Carrington and Guilding and Goulder and Spong obviously did not set out to restrict our appreciation of sacred time in Judaism and Christianity; indeed they wished (Guilding above all) to enhance our recognition of how such rhythms are basic to each. But reflexively, by cultural disposition, they reached for the most specifiable—but also the most constraining—element in any calendar, its exact sequence of readings, in order to understand the calendar itself. In doing so, their reach exceeded their grasp, because "the lectionary" of Judaism and Christianity before the fourth century in all probability has only ever existed in the minds of modern scholars.

But criticism need not—and often should not—imply complete rejection. Because Boman was not accurate in assigning where time's interval and time's rhythm are found, that does not require ignoring these two aspects of time. Because Farrer and Carrington and their followers trusted too much in lectionaries of a later period, that does not mean that festal calendars are unimportant for understanding Judaism and Christianity.[8] As we assess the rhythms of festivity in these two great religions and explore their relationships, we seek better to locate ourselves as human beings within time, and therefore better to appreciate one another.

Sacrifice and temporal mimesis

Festal calendars, including those of Judaism and Christianity, are rooted in the ancient practice of sacrifice. Before we look at the

---

[8] It is symptomatic of the capacity of an allegedly critical discipline to become as dismissive as any sectarian group that the colleagues whom Aileen Guilding herself had hired at the University of Sheffield never properly acknowledged her work after her retirement.

temporal commemoration of those feasts in the pages that follow, we need to appreciate sacrifice itself. As we understand sacrifice, we will also see that time's rhythm, time's interval are very much a part of the sacrificial process.

In a series of recent publications and public forums, I have been in dialogue with the French literary critic, René Girard.[9] Our debates with one another, some of them conducted at Stanford University (where Girard held his last appointment), have focused on the role of sacrifice in ancient cultures and its place within civilizations of the modern period. In his evaluation, sacrifice is the principal source of continuing violence in any society. In sacrifice, according to Girard, people attempt to overcome their human proclivity to covet what another person has. Rather than breaking out in contention with one another, they offer valuable commodities to a god. That god himself or herself was originally the human victim of human covetousness—a person killed by a mob—at the very beginning of any sacrificial system concerned. *Every* god was originally the victim of greed in Girard's estimation, and by offering to that victim, people try (and inevitably fail) to get beyond their greed. Because sacrifice institutionalizes greed and victims and jealousy, it simply replicates and breeds more violence in its effort to overcome it.

Scholars of religion have remained largely unconvinced by this theory. To see in every god a human victim and in every sacrifice an institutionalized crisis of greed does not do justice to the very wide variety of beliefs and practices in the ancient world as well as in modern sacrificial societies. Perhaps even more telling in its resistance to Girard's theory is the fact that modern societies which do not practice sacrifice, in terms of the ferocity of their wars and the level of their criminality, appear on the whole to be even more violent than ancient or primitive societies, where sacrifice is typically practiced.

---

[9] See Chilton, *The Temple of Jesus*, 15–25, 163–72; "René Girard, James Williams, and the Genesis of Violence," *Bulletin for Biblical Research* 3 (1993): 17–29; "The Hungry Knife: Towards a Sense of Sacrifice," in *The Bible in Human Society: Essays in Honour of John Rogerson* (ed. M. D. Carroll R., D. J. A. Clines, and P. R. Davies; Journal for the Study of the Old Testament: Supplement Series 200; Sheffield: Sheffield Academic Press, 1995): 122–38; "Sacrificial Mimesis," *Religion* 27 (1997): 225–30. As I have explained in those works, I think the best exposition of Girard's perspective is found in *The Scapegoat* (trans. Yvonne Freccero; Baltimore: Johns Hopkins University Press, 1986).

My own theory of sacrifice, based upon the earlier analysis of William Robertson Smith during the nineteenth century,[10] focuses upon the close connection between what people sacrifice and what they eat. Sacrifices the world over typically have involved preparing, offering, *and sharing* the kind and quality of food which people can only occasionally enjoy within the culture concerned. Ancient sacrifices—including the sacrifices prescribed in the Scriptures of Israel—generally involved festivity and eating amounts of food and grades of food one rarely saw. Sacrifices to appease God as a consequence of sin are only an apparent exception: their role is to reestablish the festive connection with God which sacrifice celebrates and which sin interrupts.[11] As a result, the sinner did not share in the sacrifice as one did customarily (and food ordinarily shared was assigned instead to priests or the deity), but that was in order to be able to join in regular celebration, once the festive connection with God had been established anew.

The violence inherent in sacrifice need be no greater than the violence of ordinary eating, except—of course—for the scale involved. If violence comes to be conveyed as the very meaning of sacrifice (for example, in cases of offering a human being), that is for reasons of the adjustment of the culture concerned, just as when violence becomes the center, say, of entertainment or of sexuality.

My argument with Girard over sacrifice is only of indirect concern here. What is of central interest, however, is that the dispute brings us to the issue of how sacrificial cultures, and cultures as a whole, attempt to relate human activity to the basic realities of life on which that activity is based. Both Girard and I, relying upon the insights of Aristotle, appeal to the power of *mimesis*.

The definition of that Greek word is notoriously difficult.[12] Obviously, it is the source of the terms "mimic" and "imitation" in English, but as used by Aristotle *mimesis* has a more profound

---

[10] See William Robertson Smith, *Lectures on the Religion of the Semites* (Burnett Lectures; London: Black, 1901), from the first edition of 1889, and Chilton, *The Temple of Jesus*, 6–13, 42, 45–6, 173, 176–77. Another important variant of this approach is developed by Marcel Detienne and Jean-Pierre Vernant, *The Cuisine of Sacrifice among the Greeks* (trans. Paula Wissing; Chicago: University of Chicago Press, 1989).

[11] See Leviticus 4 and Chilton, *The Temple of Jesus*, 58–60, 122.

[12] Paul Woodruff makes a typical statement in "Aristotle on Mimesis," 73–95, 89:
Aristotelian mimesis is not the same as imitation or fiction or reproduction or representation or make-believe; it is not expression; and it is not even the making of images or likenesses. Although to do some of these things may be a kind of mimesis, none of them goes to the heart of the matter.

meaning. It refers, rather, to *the human representation of an action that is perceived.* Aristotle especially used *mimesis* to explore the power of the arts to move our emotions, but it is also at the base of his understanding of science. When a person perceives a pattern in nature, one can repeat the pattern and make it more vivid, just as an actor might represent a human pattern on the stage. Whether in science or the theater, *mimesis* involves the perception and representation of patterns of action.[13]

Where it concerns sacrifice, Girard is only interested in one such pattern. He is obsessed with the moment at which people come into a covetous conflict over a single object (or rare objects), and attempt to allay their antagonism by means of mass violence. For him, the beginning and end of sacrifice is the mob. The mob kills a victim out of envy, and then deifies the victim in its collective memory, so that violence is defused in ritual myth, where it will not provoke further violence.

In my understanding, the meal is both prior to the particular kind of covetousness Girard describes and much more influential as establishing a prevailing social relationship. (I have no doubt that envy and greed have their places there, as well, but I cannot see why they should be accorded absolute privilege in explaining why people sacrifice, unless sacrifice is assumed to be evil.) Quite apart from social eating, human beings of course engage in *mimesis;* they survive and adapt in their peculiarly cerebral ways. They can eat, run, kill, hide, sleep safely, and so forth, all according to their ability to perceive and imitate activities. (They may also, apart from social eating, imitate *mimesis* itself, that is, join forces with another person or even an animal, and undertake a mimetic dialog, with or without language.) But when eating together at an ordinary table or sacrificial hearth, this mimetic activity is as much appropriated as the food. *Mimesis* determines what is eaten when, by whom, in what order, with what instruments: *mimesis* starts the game, permits its variegation, and finally it is *mimesis* which consumes and is consumed by the banqueters.

Meals are instances, not just of *mimesis* between two partners but of multipolar *mimesis,* where the possible permutations of dialog increase geometrically in proportion to the number of partners in the conversation, practiced with shared objects. Mimetic skills are heightened and indulged for their own sake, because any

---

[13] See Aryeh Kosman, "Acting: *Drama* as the *Mimesis of Praxis,*" *Essays on Aristotle's Poetics,* 51–72.

participant, in an aberrant imitation, might oneself become the object of a fresh imitation. The imperfections of mimicry themselves feed the process of multipolar *mimesis* by providing fresh activities to be imitated. Any social occasion is an instance of multipolar *mimesis;* the meal is perhaps the most basic and is certainly the most durable of such occasions.

Girard writes that "it is necessary to find the common line and the successive bifurcations that have led from the origin to the seemingly irreducible diversity of cultural forms."[14] *Mimesis,* in my opinion, is precisely the dynamism involved, and the diversity of culture is more easily explained on the basis of the *geometrical progression* of multipolar *mimesis* than it is on the basis of the merely binary variation of violence and the attempt to allay violence by means of sacrifice which Girard posits. *Mimesis* does not merely bifurcate: its power of variegation is of the essence of multipolar imitation. It is not Girard's quest for the dynamism of culture that opens him to the charge of reductionism, but his insistence that that dynamism is the binary struggle between violence and repression: "What impelled men to hunt was the search for a reconciliatory victim."[15] From my perspective, what impelled people to hunt was hunger; what taught them to hunt was the mimetic observation of animal carnivores themselves capable of learning patterns of behavior; and what produced the hunt was the social *mimesis* of that observation. Hunting is evidently a mimetic activity and violence may be a product (and therefore an occasion) of any *mimesis,* but *mimesis* is greater than hunting or violence.

It will serve to clarify the nature of *mimesis* in humans to pursue my debate with Girard. He claims, "It must have been the increasing power of imitation that initiated the process of hominization, rather than the reverse, even if the process subsequently served to accelerate that growth and made a prodigious contribution to the remarkable power of the human brain."[16] Just here, care is needed. Imitation is not unique to human beings, but unites people and animals, even certain plants. Indeed, many so-called lower forms of life are better mimics of certain phenomena than people are. They can change color, make the noises of other species, alter their physical appearances, and so forth. But people can imitate, know they

---

[14] *Things Hidden since the Foundation of the Word* (trans. Stephen Bann and Michael Metteer; Stanford: Stanford University Press, 1987), 59.

[15] Girard, *Things Hidden,* 73.

[16] Girard, *Things Hidden,* 94–5.

imitate, remember and reproduce the imitation at a later stage, imitate several models at once (in multipolar *mimesis*), arrange an imitation in language, move smoothly from imitative performance to imitative performance, and develop individual and social protocols of that movement. It is in their consciousness of *mimesis,* and in their self-conscious choice of what sorts of *mimesis* to join, that people are distinctively mimetic animals, not in their proclivity to *mimesis* itself.[17]

The common paraphrase of Aristotle, which says that "man is an imitative animal," is technically in error and misleading. A better rendering of *Poetics* 4 would be: "For to imitate is inherent in people from childhood, and in this they differ from other living things, because they are the most imitative, and learn their first lessons through imitation, and everyone enjoys imitations."[18] "Man" in the singular is not the imitative animal according to Aristotle. Only the plural of the species can be human, because a person in isolation—robbed of mimetic possibilities—is not a person. Even the collective construction of "man" misses the point that people are not distinctive in imitation, but in *mimesis*—that is, in their multipolar, conscious, and self-conscious variants of imitation. "Hominization" is not simply a matter of brain capacity, and there is no evidence that civilization as such caused people's brains to grow (as Girard seems to suggest). Rather, our mimetic and our physical potentialities have always been in relationship, and being human involves the ability to shape those potentialities.

Girard admits of the existence of "rites" among animals,[19] by which term he means behavior of a "repetitive character." His observation is limited to the formation of alliances replacing an aggressive stance between competitors with a cooperative stance. But mating, eating, hunting, and territorial staking are also instances of animal rituals. In such cases, foundations of ritual are laid bare, and it is evident that the acquisitive or covetous mimesis of which

---

[17] In a recent article entitled "Mutation, Selection, and Vertical Transmission of Theistic Memes in Religious Canons," *Journal of Memetics* 5 (2001), John Gottsch argues that hominization began with the need of large apes to be physically self-aware in order to negotiate the demands of living in trees. He then sees an exponential leap in mimetic capacity with the development of speech. I would see consciousness and self-consciousness (as distinct from physical self-awareness) as part of the latter development. I am obliged to Dr. Gottsch for letting me see his article in manuscript.

[18] For a discussion, see Chilton, *The Temple of Jesus,* 164–65.

[19] Girard, *Things Hidden,* 98.

Girard speaks need not be posited as the grounding cause of ritual. By referring to "acquisitive mimesis" as leading to "conflictual mimesis," and then on to violence on a sacrificial scale,[20] Girard implicitly acknowledges that his interest focuses on only a particular aspect of *mimesis* generally. It is true—and useful—to understand as Girard clearly does that such conflict loses sight of the originating object, and feeds on itself, transferring its putative target. But that susceptibility to rapid development, from one moment of imitation to another, is of the genius of *mimesis,* not of conflictual *mimesis* alone. Social "life," that primal metaphor at the heart of "the social sciences," is precisely the generation and replication and mutation of imitative gestures in visual, auditory, and physical terms. People even try to smell the same, but different.

Mimesis is what occasions sacrifice, where the products of *mimesis* are given and consumed, and what generates those functions of culture which constitute civilization. Precisely because *mimesis* is crucial in such a fundamentally positive sense, Girard can write of Jesus: "the word that comes from God, the word that enjoins us to imitate no one but God, the God who refrains from all forms of reprisal and makes his sun shine upon the 'just' and the 'unjust' without distinction—this word remains, for him, absolutely valid."[21] Unmistakably, Girard juxtaposes Jesus' *mimesis* with Satan's, "the religion that comes from man . . . as opposed to the religion that comes from God."[22]

Because Girard's account of revelation really amounts to a different sort of *mimesis* from that of covetous greed, his contention that people can be released from *mimesis* altogether is misleading.[23] Even the bifurcation of *mimesis* into "good" and "bad," another feature of his analysis in his later work, is only practicable when activity is judged from the perspective of social values, which are themselves generated by *mimesis.* For that reason, a better approach is to define *mimesis* as an undifferentiated activity and to pose the moral question only when what I call the "arc" or trajectory of *mimesis* is at issue. Violence and work, for example, are both mimetic phenomena; indeed they can and often do coexist within a single, social action by a group of people. The challenge of a mimetic analysis is to show where *mimesis* degrades into violence and in what the degradation consists.

---

[20] Girard, *Things Hidden,* 26.
[21] Girard, *Things Hidden,* 206.
[22] Girard, *Things Hidden,* 166.
[23] Girard, *Things Hidden,* 36, 178–79, 197, 206, 219, 277.

In Girard's scheme, greed is always the culprit, that is, the mechanism in which the other who possesses an object is taken as a rival, an obstacle to be overcome. That Girard has identified a possible source of aggression may readily be admitted, and his assessment of how individuals' aggression might become social violence is illuminating. But two reservations remain: (1) whatever its merits as an analysis of violence, Girard's approach to religion is too bound by the modern assumption that sacrifice is harmful, and (2) his claims in regard to the New Testament, as being exclusively revelatory, are unsupported. In other words, I accept much of what Girard says in regard to violence, but neither his identification of violence with sacrifice nor his assertion of the unique value of the Christian canon to remove violence strikes me as tenable.

The New Testament for him reveals the way of love, the only viable alternative to violence. But the fact is that biblically, within the Johannine literature, which is so dear to Girard, *mimesis* is understood as the instrument of salvation: "Beloved, we are now God's children, and it has not yet been made manifest what we shall be; we know that when it has been made manifest, we shall be like unto him, because we shall see him as he is" (1 John 3:2). The Johannine postulation of the *imitatio Dei* and *imitatio Christi* is consistent with characteristically biblical ethics, and involves not the displacement of *mimesis* but the reconstitution of *mimesis*.

Mimesis may devolve into rivalry, sometimes in the interests of acquisition, as Girard suggests. (Whether acquisition is solely the result of a desire to be "the Other" in each case is, however, open to question.) But *mimesis* and rivalry may thrive independently of desired objects. Indeed, Girard makes desire "the mimetic crisis in itself,"[24] thereby denigrating desire in almost puritanical, albeit post-Calvinist, terms. I would suggest that desire is more basically the impulse to imitate, in that imitation, concupiscence, or greed—the Augustinian category Girard is actually describing—might turn the dynamic of *mimesis* into the vicious cycle of appropriation which Girard so lucidly characterizes. But at this stage we can suspect that the literary doubles of the nineteenth century (above all in Dostoyevski and Stendahl) have too far influenced Girard's basic definition of *mimesis,* which is indeed—biblically evaluated—internally flawed but not beyond redemption. When rivalry becomes

[24] Girard, *Things Hidden,* 288.

the universe of *mimesis,* rather than the reverse, the possibility emerges that there is such a thing as being too bound to what Girard calls "double business."[25]

Aristotle conceived of *mimesis* in terms sufficiently universal to account for its operation within humanity as a whole: "Because things imitated imitate human activities, which are necessarily excellent or base, since practically all dispositions follow along these lines, for all dispositions differ in being wicked and noble" (*Poetics* 2 [1448ª 1–5]).[26] The gestures we perform differ from one another, and the means and manner of an imitation are also distinguishing features.

His emphasis upon reason (*nous*) led Aristotle to abandon *mimesis* as the fundamental category of human behavior in the *Nichomachean Ethics,* but it is not difficult to see the form a more consistently mimetic Aristotelianism would take. As a matter of fact, it is arguable that the substance of Aristotle's ethical theory really is mimetic, rather than simply rational. The human good which is the purpose of the theory "becomes an exercise of the soul in accordance with virtue" (*Nicomachean Ethics* I.7). Those virtues, in turn, are seen as habits which "we get by first exercising them, as also happens in the case of the other arts as well" (*Nicomachean Ethics* II.1). Clearly, that is a conscious description of human *mimesis* that is fully in line with the *Poetics.* But once rational choice comes into the picture, the emphasis falls upon reason's commitment to the mean of moderation between excess and defect in which virtue is held to reside. It is nonetheless indicative of his substantially mimetic explanation of ethics that Aristotle expatiates upon the mutuality of friendship as the ideal model of virtuous activity (*Nicomachean Ethics* VIII.3–14). The mimetic dialog between friends is the foundation and sustenance of their character. That social focus even serves as transitional to the subject of the *Politics,* where Aristotle's mimetic model of behavior is worked out in communal terms. It is also telling that "reason" is for Aristotle more a criterion of selection among mimetic options than such an option in itself.

Girard's approach is of fundamental importance in challenging the Aristotelian notion of what is imitated in *mimesis.* Where Aristotle has us imitating activities, Girard has us disputing over ob-

---

[25] See "To Double Business Bound," in *Essays on Literature, Mimesis, and Anthropology* (Baltimore: Johns Hopkins University Press, 1978).

[26] See D. W. Lucas, *Aristotle, Poetics* (Oxford: Clarendon, 1972).

jects. As has already been suggested, the equation of *mimesis*, rivalry, and violence is too simple. Each may lead to the next, but that does not make them equivalents, even functionally speaking. Nonetheless, Girard forces us to recognize that the *mimesis* involving objects is functionally distinct from the *mimesis* involving gestures alone. Acts are limitless; things are not. Indeed, a certain practice of pragmatic *mimesis* may be said to constitute the invention of property.

Moreover, a focus on the question of *mimesis* as the issue that underlies ethics explains what Aristotle's reason alone cannot: his own relentless interest in social activities as both the origin and the target of discourse. A society may be defined as a constellation of routines of *mimesis* focused in and through pragmatic objects within a larger process of mimetic dialogue.

The larger process of mimetic dialogue includes communal notions of time. Within the practice and the perspective of sacrificial routine, calendars emerge which attest precisely the two coordinates of time we have been specifying: the rhythm of recurrence and the interval of sequence. Girard's contribution invites us to ask: is our dilemma about time's constraint and time's vacancy a result of commodifying time? We now dispute over who owns our time, when it is time itself that gives us birth.

The rhythm of the sacrifice and the rhythm of the seasons are directly related, and the interval of one year in distinction to another is what distinguishes the annual pattern as annual. In other words, the mimetic process which sacrifice brings to social articulation is also the engine of calendars and of time itself. Rhythm is basic to the perception and performance of temporal *mimesis,* and interval is what permits a rhythmic pattern to be set in distinction from others. This underlying pattern of *mimesis,* articulating human actions and emotions and meanings, is what frames our religious life, including the calendars of sacrificial time. As we look to the wisdom of ancient calendars of Judaism and Christianity, the dynamism of that *mimesis* will especially draw our attention.

CHAPTER THREE

Festal Judaism

A calendar produced out of the crucible of time

The festivals of Israel mark out a deep involvement with the agricultural rhythm of the land set aside by God for his people. That land features as the central, organizing principle of Judaism's calendar. The book of Leviticus, the principal representative of the Priestly source within the Torah, speaks of those who occupied the land before the Israelites as being "vomited out," for the precise reason that they did not observe rules of sexual purity required by God (so Leviticus 18:24–30). Purity was the means by which Israel, then, could stay in the land; inheritance of the covenantal promise of the land was conditional upon faithfulness to the purity of the covenant.[1]

The laws of cleanness are Israel's means of maintaining a solidarity with God through sacrifice, apart from which the land cannot be retained. The land, in Leviticus, is not for Israel; Israel is for the

---

[1] Dietary purity was maintained along two basic lines. First, parts of normally pure animals, such as blood and fat, were to be assigned to God alone in sacrifice, and therefore could not be consumed by human beings. Blood and fat were not inherently impure; belonging to God alone, they were *too holy* for human consumption.

Second, other animals, impure beasts and carcasses, were not fit for any consumption—human or divine—because they did not belong with the divine order of creation. An impure animal was seen as a monstrous hybrid which God had not mandated within the orders of creation; hybridity, indeed, is a principal danger in sexual transgression. Carcasses are impure because they, too, are bodies that do not belong to the orders of life.

These two different strands of purity/impurity are woven into a single imperative to maintain purity.

service of God in his land, because that land has been set aside to supply pure sacrifice according to his orders of creation.[2]

The Priestly source (conventionally known as "P") is by no means the earliest material in the Torah (or Pentateuch). A consensus of scholarship places P's composition during the fifth century B.C.E.[3] The Pentateuch as we know it was completed during that time, with the addition of this specifically Priestly source, which provides direction for the conduct of sacrificial worship as well as for producing and preparing offerings. With the emergence of the Pentateuch (the five books attributed to Moses), an ideal Israel, founded upon the regulations of Moses, emerged as a truly canonical standard. Torah was now written, and it offered a key for the constitution of Israel.

The materials within the Priestly source were, of course, not simply invented during the fifth century. Earlier sources had already been composed. During the tenth century B.C.E., the temple Solomon constructed had become a new intellectual and cultural center in Israel and therefore a focus of the codification of tradition. In addition to the "Court History," an account of David's reign composed shortly after his death (2 Samuel 9–1 Kings 2), the source within the Pentateuch that scholars call "J" was produced. J (named after its putative author or authors, collectively called the "Yahwist" [earlier spelled with a "J" in the Latin manner]) first linked, in literary form, the people of the Davidic kingdom with creation, the patriarchs, the exodus, and the possession of the land. From the outset, God is known as "Yahweh" in this source.

Earlier, shorter books had been compiled to be recited at cultic centers, so that a treaty, or regulations of purity or ethics, or alleged genealogical connections, or victories and other formative events might be remembered in association with sacrifice at any cultic center. But Jerusalem became the preeminent sacrificial center under the protection of the Davidic dynasty, and that involved the collection of these materials during the tenth century in an

---

[2] For a full discussion, see Chilton, "Sacrifice in 'Classic' Israel," in *The Temple of Jesus*, 45–67.

[3] See B. A. Levine, "Priestly Writers," *The Interpreter's Dictionary of the Bible, Supplementary Volume* (ed. K. Crim; Nashville: Abingdon, 1976), 683–87. Jacob Milgrom has championed the view that the source must be dated much earlier; see "Priestly ('P') Source," *Anchor Bible Dictionary* (ed. D. N. Freedman; 6 vols.; New York: Doubleday, 1992), 5:454–61. I would of course agree that much of what it says goes back to the period of the first temple, but the Aramaisms of "P" suggest it was produced during the Persian period.

early attempt to present them more coherently, for use in the temple (and the royal court) during the feasts which were primarily celebrated there.

After Solomon's death, united Israel was divided in 922 B.C.E. into Israel in the north and Judah in the south. The book of Kings lays the blame for that division on Solomon's apostasy (1 Kings 11:29–40), and there is a thematic link in Scripture between marriage to non-Israelite women and idolatry. But the kings, both north and south, undermined their own authority by their recourse to slavery and their conspicuous consumption, not only by their idolatry. The last aspect is nonetheless an especial feature in the careers of the worst kings. During the ninth century B.C.E., Ahab in the north with his Phoenician wife Jezebel fomented the worship of Baal and was opposed by the prophet Elijah (1 Kings 16:29–22:40); and in the south during the eighth century, Ahaz renovated the temple to look like the one in Damascus, and may even have practiced human sacrifice (2 Kings 16:1–20). It is evident that the alliance of Ahab with Tyre and of Ahaz with Damascus was a formative influence in their respective religious policies.

Prophecy found its voice as a movement in its opposition to the monarchs it regarded as apostate. Prior to the crystallizing impact of that opposition, prophets appear to have been identified as those who spoke for God, often in association with worship in particular sanctuaries. Their prophetic ministry might, to a greater or lesser extent, involve unusual states of consciousness and/or atypical behavior, sometimes with the use of music and dance. But first the association with David, and then the antagonism of kings in the north and south made of prophecy a surprisingly coherent movement. The first evidence of prophecy as a literary genre in ancient Israel involves the eighth-century prophet Amos. Cycles of stories about prophets and their teachings (for example, Deborah, Elijah, and Elisha) circulated before that time, but the collection of Amos' oracles into a coherent message marks a pivotal phase in the development of Israel's Scriptures. Fundamentally a prophet of doom against the northern kingdom, Amos foretold judgment against Israel's apostate kings, and Hosea vividly generalized that theme to include the nation as a whole. Micah and Isaiah followed them in the south, and an urgent appeal for social justice became a hallmark of prophecy there.

The doom announced against the north by an Amos or a Hosea must have appeared an idle prophecy during periods of prosperity, but when, in 722 B.C.E., the capital of the north was taken by the Assyrians, the climax of Israel's subjection to a policy of subjugation and exile, the prophetic message appeared to be vindicated. The works of the northern prophets were preserved in the south, together with another source of the Pentateuch known as "E" (for the "Elohist," after the generic name "God," Elohim, in Hebrew). The E source also tells the story of Israel's beginnings, but with a northern slant.

The Elohist source portrays God as revealing his personal name to Moses alone, so that beforehand he was known as "Elohim," God. The mountain of Moses' revelation is known as Horeb, rather than Sinai, and there are alternative versions of stories known in J, and some new stories; in addition, the conception of God is markedly less anthropomorphic. Clearly, there were those in the north—priests and prophets and scribes—who opposed the royal attempt at syncretism. Nonetheless, the attacks the canonical prophets direct against other, deceitful prophets, and against the cultic hypocrisy of some priests are eloquent testimony to the power of the opposition and its support among both prophetic and priestly groups.

Spurred on by the demise of Israel in the north, whose people were lost to history, the prophets in Judah attempted to purify the life of their people. Isaiah urgently argued against foreign alliances and insisted that fidelity to God alone would save Jerusalem; Jeremiah ceaselessly denounced faithlessness, and was imprisoned for his trouble (see Jeremiah 20; 37); Ezekiel's announcements and enactments of coming disaster won him the mockery of his contemporaries (see Ezekiel 33:30). But in the reign of Josiah, a royal reformation backed much of the critique of the prophets (cf. 2 Kings 22:1–23:30; 2 Chronicles 34:1–35:27).

Josiah changed worship in the temple to accord with covenantal norms; he centralized sacrifice, even of the *Pesach* (Passover), in Jerusalem; he tolerated no foreign incursions. His program was guided by a scroll of the law found in the temple during the restoration—a scroll that has, since antiquity (and the scholarship of St. Jerome in particular), been associated with the present book of Deuteronomy. That book presses an agenda of radical centralization and separation from foreign nations, such as impelled Josiah. But in 609 B.C.E., Josiah was killed in battle in an attempt to thwart a military expedition by Pharaoh Neco and the Assyrians at the strategic location called Megiddo. The impact of his death may be gauged by the impact of that name upon the apocalyptic tradition, in the form "Armageddon" (Revelation 16:16, cf. Zechariah 12:11).

The end of the kingdom of Judah came quickly after the death of Josiah. Culminating in 587 B.C.E., the Babylonian empire, which had succeeded the Assyrians (cf. the book of Nahum), implemented a policy of exile, subsequent to their siege of Jerusalem and their destruction of the temple. Had the course of events then followed what happened to Israel in the north, there would today be no Judaism to study. Paradoxically, however, just the forces which must have seemed sure to destroy the religion of the covenant with Yawheh instead assured its survival and nurtured its international dimension. During the Babylonian exile, the priestly and prophetic movements joined forces to form a united program of restoration that put a form of Israel back on the map within a generation. Even more influentially, they memorialized their vision of that Israel in a book and made it classic for their successors.

The Josian reforms had already allied some priests with some prophets, and the priests played a central part in the formation of "classic" Israel. Priestly/prophetic scribes redacted "D," the source of the Pentateuch in tune with the message of Deuteronomy, together with "J" and "E." That work, probably completed during the sixth century, was slightly later combined with what is known as the "Deuteronomic History" (the books Joshua, Judges, 1–2 Samuel, and 1–2 Kings), a recounting of events between Moses and the exile which explains success or failure according to the nation's adherence to the program that drove Josiah. The Pentateuch came to the form in which we would recognize it during the fifth century, when the source called "P" supplemented the earlier traditions of the Torah and provided the whole with the editorial framework of the five books of Moses.

The dispossession of Judah to Babylon, then, set up the priestly and prophetic hegemony that made restoration possible. But just as "P" sets out particularly priestly concerns, the prophetic movement also brought a distinctive message to the canon. The prophets generally agreed with their priestly confederates that the land was to be possessed again, and postexilic additions to the books of Isaiah (40–55), Jeremiah (23:1–8; 31), and Ezekiel (40–48) constitute powerful visions of (and incentives for) return. But the previous abuses of the kings and their sanctuaries made the prophetic movement insist that righteousness was the prior requirement of sacrifice, and that the events of the recent past were a warning.

Zechariah might be happy to set out the hope of a priestly messiah beside the Davidic king who was to rule (chapters 3 and 4), but
even so the predominant emphasis fell upon the crucial necessity of
loyalty to the worship of God (see Zechariah 14). Moreover, escha-
tology became characteristic of the prophetic movement, both in
additions to biblical prophets, such as Isaiah and Ezekiel, and in
fresh works, such as Joel and Malachi. The contemporary gover-
nance—whether Persian (from 539 B.C.E.), Alexandrine (from 332
B.C.E.), Ptolemaic (from 323 B.C.E.), or Seleucid (from 200 B.C.E.)—
and the present temple were provisional, until an anointed king
and an anointed priest would rule properly. The image of a priestly
orientation redefined by the prophets is projected into the career of
Ezra in the books of Ezra and Nehemiah: prophet, priest, and
scribe become one in their insistence on the vision of classic Israel,
centered upon the restored temple.

The calendar that was inscribed in the emergent Pentateuch is
dedicated to time as recurring, marked out by the seasons of the agricultural year. But this dedication to recurrence was enhanced and
made poignant by the catastrophic, recent proof that the people of
Israel might prove to remain only an interval of time on the land.
God might "vomit out" even them. That startling image evokes a
visceral sense of living on the edge of the interval of time: there
were people banned from God's land before, and even Israel might
be banned (again, see Leviticus 18:24–30). Observing recurrence
and maintaining Israel's identity on the edge of time's interval are
therefore woven together within the biblical calendar. Only memory can enable Israel to know itself, to be familiar with and to realize the purity that keeps it from the abominations of those things
which never should have been done with God's creation, as well as
from those elements (blood and fat) so sacred they belong only to
God. Because the issues of both kinds of purity—the purity distinguishing Israel from the nations as well as the purity safely
separating Israel from God—especially need realization when the
land is harvested of its plant and animal produce; festivals are
moments when the recurrence of the seasons and the interval of
Israel's time as Israel come sharply into focus.

Harvests

Each major festival is at base a week or so of harvest: in the
spring, in the summer, in the autumn. Spring brings early grain, es-

pecially barley, and is also time to move the flocks on from one pasture to another. Summer sees the larger grain-harvest of wheat. Autumn is the last time of gathering for the cycle, and the grapes and olives and nuts of that season make it the most joyous time of all.

Although the calendar of ancient Israel developed with profoundly theological explanations of these recurring festivals and in the addition of other feasts, fasts, and commemorative moments, the primacy of agricultural practice and experience needs to be recollected throughout, if one is to appreciate the sense of the calendar and the genuine joy and enjoyment involved in the festivals.[4] The fundamental importance of the three great agricultural festivals is signaled by the requirement that every male of Israel appear before the Lord every year at these times (Exodus 23:14–17; 34:23; Deuteronomy 16:16–17). That is, of course, an idealized expectation, but it enables us to appreciate how deeply felt was the connection between the rhythm of the fields and the rhythm of God's choice of Israel. It could be felt in city, town, and country, wherever the biblical calendar was known.

Each of the major festivals has its own character, and over time would generate its own explanation in terms of the remembrance of the intervals which formed the understanding of Israel. Spring (Passover) corresponded to the exodus, summer (Weeks) to the giving of the covenant, and autumn *(Sukkoth)* to the sojourn in the wilderness which brought Israel to its land.[5] But the fact of harvest in each case gives the festival a communal, celebratory, and sacrificial character.

The greater and richer the harvest, the more intense and cooperative the work of any agricultural commune must be. That demands a social structure at the local scale, and the hard labor of harvesting was basically undertaken by the Israelites themselves: slavery does not appear to have been a major institution until the monarchy, and even then had more to do with building and service

---

[4] See F. Rochber-Halton, "Calendars," *Anchor Bible Dictionary,* 1:810–14; James C. VanderKam, "Calendars, Ancient Israelite and Early Jewish," *Anchor Bible Dictionary,* 1:814–20; J. Mann, "The Observance of the Sabbath and the Festivals in the First Two Centuries of the Current Era according to Philo, Josephus, the New Testament and the Rabbinic Sources," *The Jewish Review* 4 (1914): 433–56, 498–532; and H. Schauss, *The Jewish Festivals: History and Observance* (trans. S. Jaffe; New York: Schocken, 1962).

[5] See Chilton, "Judaism," *Dictionary of Jesus and the Gospels* (ed. J. B. Green, S. McKnight, I. H. Howard; Downers Grove, Ill.: InterVarsity, 1992), 398–405.

than with agriculture. A primary motivation in this communal work was the urgency of harvest. Once ripe, a crop must be taken in quickly, with as little waste and damage as possible, if the full benefit is to be enjoyed. One way to enjoy the crop is to share some of it (indeed, a great deal of it) at the time of harvest itself. That celebration leads naturally to sacrifice, a moment when Israel gathers with Israel's God to consume with pleasure and generosity what God permits to be produced on God's land.

Passover/*Pesach* (Limping)

The spring festival as a whole included *Pesach* proper and the Feast of Unleavened Bread. But the festival generally came to be called *Pesach,* as is attested by the end of the first century by Josephus (*Jewish Antiquities* 17 § 213; 20 § 106). Earlier, when he wrote *The Jewish War,* he tended to distinguish the two festivals (see *The Jewish War* 2 § 280; 6 §§ 423–424). The historical association of *Pesach* with the exodus from Egypt, the principal interval in the remembrance of what makes Israel, is dominant to this day and has been since the presentation of the feast in Exodus 12. That link was only strengthened during the rabbinic period, when the memory of the exodus eclipses a sense of agricultural practice (see the mishnaic tractate *Pesachim* 10:5). But the term *pesach* basically means "limping" (or "skipping," as some scholars more delicately express the same kind of movement), and it referred initially to the limping of the spring lamb (a male yearling), hobbled prior to its being slaughtered, sacrificed, and eaten. This designation intimates the sense of the feast of *Pesach* prior to its almost complete identification with the events of the exodus.

Several of the associations of this feast and Unleavened Bread evidence the deep connection which was felt between the act of eating in Israel and the practice of sacrifice. It was a regular practice in Israel throughout the year not to eat the sinew on the inside of the hip (see Genesis 32:32); the reason for that seems to be that the animal was bound or wounded there before it was killed, much as the angel hobbled Jacob during their wrestling. The ritual dance of those who took part in the sacrifice of the spring yearling could be designated by the term *pesach,* as could the entire festival. The dance and the sacrifice imitated one another. Killing a lamb in spring prior to moving on to new pastures produced an early benefit of the extensive organization required to shepherd flocks, and provided an occasion for the gathering of shepherd communities, even before Israel possessed its land. It is striking that Jacob, a rich shepherd at this point in Genesis, is given the name of Israel for struggling with God (Genesis 32:28), that he is caused to limp in his wrestling, and that his injury is directly connected to the Israelite practice of not eating the sinew on the inside of the hip (Genesis 32:24–32). Here we have an image of Israel before the possession of the land: the struggle with God is linked to the consumption from the flock and the blessings that are promised.

The pastoral festival of *Pesach* seems already to have been an Israelite tradition during the period in Egypt. Indeed, Moses declares to Pharaoh the desire to sacrifice as the motivation for what at first was to be a temporary departure into the wilderness, in order to offer in a way Egyptians would find objectionable (so Exodus 5:1; 8:8, 25–32). That departure, in a sequence of events remembered as constituting national Israel, proved to be definitive, and the events of *Pesach* and Unleavened Bread in that sense came to dominate over the meaning of the spring festival, at least for those who composed the Scriptures (see Exodus 12): now it is Yahweh who misses a step when he comes to the houses of the Israelites (Exodus 12:23, 27), and the lack of yeast in the bread is a sign of Israel's haste in departing (Exodus 12:34).

The persistent celebration of *Pesach* in households (authorized in Exodus 12:3–4) rather than in the central temple in Jerusalem, reflects the deep roots of the festival, both in the history of Israel and in the affections of those who kept the practice. But under the reign of King Josiah (see 2 Kings 23:21–23; 2 Chronicles 35:1–19; and Deuteronomy 16:1–8), a determined and largely successful attempt was made to centralize the feast, by arranging for the sacrifice of the animals in the temple prior to their distribution for consumption in Jerusalem alone. The animals at issue now are not only lambs, but bulls as well, in keeping with the more elite celebration in the wealthier, national Israel that is envisaged. The temple was destroyed soon after Josiah's reform (in 587 B.C.E.), but the process of canonizing Scriptures favored the close association between *Pesach* and the temple. As a result, rabbinic practice, established after the second destruction of the temple in 70 C.E., does not include the consumption of lamb and distinguishes itself from "the *Pesach* of Egypt" (see *Pesachim* 9:5). Still, the possibility of local observance of the festival as set out in Exodus 12 both before and after the destruction of the temple cannot be excluded, and even the description of Josiah's reform includes the notice that there were priests who did not eat unleavened bread in Jerusalem but preferred to do so locally (2 Kings 23:9). To this day, Samaritan Judaism keeps the sacrifice of Passover on Mount Gerizim.[6]

Unleavened Bread

Pesach in ancient Israel was the prelude to the Feast of Unleavened Bread. During that feast, the first grain of the year (barley for the most part) was consumed, and without yeast. The removal of yeast, and its eventual replacement with fresh yeast, carried a practical benefit. Yeast acts as an agent in fermentation, and its effects are passed on; that is, yeasted dough, introduced into new dough, will result in leavened bread. But although the process carries on, after many generations of bread the agency of the yeast is weakened (owing, it is now thought, to contamination by other strains of yeast or by other microorganisms[7]). So yearly renewal is beneficial, a fresh start with new yeast of proven quality. By timing that removal and renewal at the time of the spring grain, Israel also enjoys its first harvest, without the usual intervention of leavening.

Grain unleavened was in any case the only way in which cereal could be offered to God in sacrifice (see Leviticus 2:11; 6:17), and yeast as such was prohibited in connection with direct offering to God (Exodus 23:18; 34:25), so the Feast of Unleavened Bread was a period in which Israel consumed grain in the way that God was held to. Just as the lamb of *Pesach* came to be associated with the exodus, so did the Unleavened Bread. Rabbinic practice (see *Mishnah Pesachim* 1:1–4) emphasizes the removal of leaven within each household in Israel, and that serves to retain the original, domestic sensibility of *Pesach* and Unleavened Bread. What survives within rabbinic practice is non-sacrificial, in that the destruction of the temple makes genuinely cultic offering impossible; but the rabbinic prescriptions are also irreducibly domestic, and to that extent they are an interesting reversion to the conception of Exodus 12.

---

[6] See Reinhard Pummer, *The Samaritans* (Iconography of Religions 25.5; Leiden: Brill, 1987).

[7] See R. Y. Stanier et al., *The Microbial World* (Englewood Cliffs, N.J.: Prentice-Hall, 1986).

The time of *Pesach*

The Mishnah reflects a keen sense of the importance of getting the time of *Pesach* right. Its placement not only determines the keeping of that feast, but calibrates the festal year as a whole. Indeed, that calibration may be said to convey what is distinctive about the Judaic calendar. The system of reckoning the year is predicated upon planting and harvesting. So the first harvest, *Pesach,* controls the whole annual cycle.

The month in which *Pesach* fell (Nisan[8]) began, as do all months, with the new moon. That assures that the coming of *Pesach,* on sundown after the fourteenth day of the month, corresponds to the full moon (truly, a harvest moon). There is an interesting correspondence between the day which commences with darkness, and the dark of the new moon which begins every month. Both are related to the understanding that God created in darkness, that light was his first creative gift (see Genesis 1:1–3). The annual calendar also begins in the time of relative darkness, winter. So the first month, *Pesach*'s month, starts in the spring.

Spring is calculated by the sun's course. When the spring equinox arrives, that is spring by the solar calendar. By Israel's reckoning, Nisan begins with the first new moon after the equinox of spring. Although this calculation is not complicated, coordination is obviously important, and the Mishnah imagines that the observation of the new moon should be made in Jerusalem, considered the center of the disk-shaped earth. A system of bonfires (*Mishnah Rosh Hashanah* 2:2–4), starting outward from Jerusalem, would alert Israel and the Jewish world to the dawn of the new year and its first feast.

The beginning of the year once involved setting aside a yearling lamb for consumption at *Pesach,* but that practice changed with the introduction of Josiah's reform of the feast as a festival of the temple. Anyone who adhered to the teaching of Deuteronomy would see to the presentation of a lamb or bull in Jerusalem; only someone who lived in a reasonable traveling distance would present his own animal. *The Gospel according to Thomas* 60 (following the conventional enumeration of the sayings) refers to Jesus

---

[8] The names of the months are postexilic: Nisan, Iyyar, Sivan, Tammuz, Av, Elul, Tishri, Cheshvan, Kislev, Tevet, Shevat, Adar. They derive from the Babylonian calendar; see Ephraim Jehudah Wiesenberg, "Calendar," *Encyclopedia Judaica* (16 vols.; Jerusalem: Keter, 1978), 5:43–50, and VanderKam, "Calendars," 1:814–20.

calling attention to a Samaritan carrying a lamb, presumably to the temple—an unusual act for the distance involved as well as for the person who was showing such devotion. Samaritan practice to this day is centered on Mount Gerizim, and the ordinary estrangement between Jews and Samaritans during the first century is well known (see John 4:9). *Pesach* was a centralized feast by the first century, although the possibility cannot be ruled out that some Jews followed the teaching of Exodus 12 and kept *Pesach* at home. After all, deep divisions among members of the high priestly class had even resulted in the establishment of an alternative temple in Egypt during the second century C.E.: there was no shortage of alternative practices within early Judaism when it came to sacrificial issues.

Indeed, even the calendar itself was challenged. The pseudepigraphical book of *Jubilees* sets out a comprehensive alternative to the combined lunar and solar calendar of most forms of Judaism. Rejecting the lunar months, which are such a prominent feature of the calendar in the Pentateuch, *Jubilees* provided for twelve non-lunar months of thirty days. An additional day was added to each of the four seasons, to yield a solar calendar of 364 days, with the major feasts all falling on the same day of the year.[9] The seventh day, the seventh year, and the jubilee cycles of seven times seven years are calibrated to the sun alone.

This radical break with what had been and would continue to be a practical compromise of lunar and solar elements was to have profound consequences. Solar enthusiasts championed their uniquely sun-based calendar of feasts during the early Maccabean period,[10] while it still seemed possible that the Maccabees would provide for that calendar and attendant concerns in the restored temple. When they did not, their head was labeled "the wicked priest" in the Essene theology which is attested by the Dead Sea Scrolls.

The question which emerges, of course, is why such a radical shift should have been proposed. The circumstances of the second century B.C.E., which brought the Maccabees to power, largely explain adherence to the solar calendar and the larger tendency to which it belonged. James VanderKam has shown that biblical sources with priestly ties referred to months not by name but by

---

[9] See O. S. Wintermute, "Jubilees," *The Old Testament Pseudepigrapha* (ed. J. H. Charlesworth; 2 vols.; Garden City, N.Y.: Doubleday, 1983–1985), 2:39.

[10] Wintermute ("Jubilees") suggests between 161 and 140 B.C.E.

number. Further, the most detailed schedule of feasts, in addition to special offerings at the start of each month, is attested "in the priestly parts of the Pentateuch":[11]

Pesach	1/14, with selection of the lamb on 1/10
Unleavened Bread	1/15–21
Second *Pesach* (for those unclean the previous month)	2/14
Weeks	3[12]
"Day of Solemn Rest" (later called New Year; see below)	7/1
Day of Atonement	7/10
Tabernacles/Booths	7/15–21

Precise concern for timing is evident here, as is an aversion to the Babylonian names of months (see Ezra, Nehemiah, Esther, and Zechariah, as well as rabbinic literature). The solar calendar is the next step beyond the program of the Priestly source, and was probably first developed in Babylonia after the Pentateuch, to some extent in order to distinguish Israel's calendar from the Babylonian system. By the third century, it is attested in *1 Enoch*. The accommodation of the Jerusalem priesthood to the Seleucids, and then the desecration of the temple, brought the priestly adherents of the solar calendar to attempt a calendrical reformation of the cult. They never succeeded, but the vigor of their effort is reflected in the Dead Sea Scrolls and in other documents produced by priestly militants.

The failure of the attempt was as spectacular as the difference between the Essenes and the preponderance of Jewish practice. Adherents of the lunar element of the calendar were also, of course, sabbatarians. The Sabbath, the seventh day, broke the lunar month into quarters of the moon, since the start of each month was the new moon (as the Pentateuch provides). The sequence of sabbath years and jubilee years derives from that, as in the proportionate measurement of seven weeks between *Pesach* and Weeks. The rigid emphasis upon the repetitive seven in the strictly solar calendar misses the sense of recurrence which an observation of the moon's phases facilitates. Lunar observation makes the progress of the

---

[11] See VanderKam, "Calendars," 1:814–20, 815–16.
[12] On the problem of specifying the day, even in the Priestly source, see VanderKam, "Calendars," 1:816.

month, Sabbath by Sabbath, easier to trace and more palpable than an abstract counting does. The combination of lunar and solar principles that the Bible and the rabbis embraced coordinates Israel's celebration with the harvests, which God provides his people within creation, in a way that his people could follow with the most obvious change in the sky at night.

Although the battle to determine the calendar of Israel in the period of the Maccabees may seem to have been abstruse, in fact deeply opposing apprehensions of time were at odds within the conflict.

The solar calendar was committed to the interval in which Israel lived. The book of *Jubilees* pictured a precise unrolling of years corresponding to the requirements of sabbath day, sabbath year, and sabbath of the sabbath year (the Jubilee), until the jubilee of the jubilees would bring time itself to an end. The interval involved was enormous, involving the starting point and ending point of creation, but the only time that finally mattered was the time that counted out the interval before the end, the full redemption of Israel. During that interval, keeping time correctly mattered: an accurately kept *Pesach* would ward off the plagues such as afflicted Egypt (*Jubilees* 49:15, see also 6:32–38).

The conventional calendar, a compromise of lunar and solar elements, commits itself to recurrence, and does not specify the interval within which Israel lives. For that reason, the solar calendar comported with the apocalypticism of the Essenes, while the solar-lunar calendar was accepted by the Maccabees, as well as by the priests who supported them (the Sadducees) and the Pharisees who lived in a much more uneasy, sometimes even violent, relationship with them.

The Pharisees, who called themselves sages and were widely known as rabbis, ultimately produced the Mishnah at the end of the second century. The mishnaic tractate *Pesachim* sets out clear provisions for *Pesach* in the conditions after the Romans destroyed the temple in 70 C.E. As actually kept, the emphasis of the feast falls on the Seder (the "order" of the meal) of unleavened bread, as we have already seen. But the Mishnah also specifies how and when the paschal sacrifice is to occur in Israel and the Diaspora.

By that stage, apocalypticism, particularly in the activist form that had produced two failed and disastrous revolts against Rome, had been largely discredited within Judaism. Moreover, the burning of the temple under Vespasian and Titus, and then the demolition of the temple and the banning of Jews from Jerusalem under Hadrian, meant that the mainspring of the calendar—sacrificial worship in accordance with the Torah—could no longer be carried out.

The Mishnah reflects the pharisaic-rabbinic response, which was to a significant extent expressed in terms of time. The mishnaic tractate which actually explains how the time of *Pesach* is to be set is not *Pesachim* (which principally deals with the feast as the once again domesticated festival of unleavening), but *Rosh Hashanah*, "New Year." In other words, the Mishnah reflects a recalibration of the year in rabbinic Judaism, to make a new start of the annual recurrence of Israel's existence.

In the provisions of the Pentateuch, a "Day of Solemn Rest" was to commence the seventh month (Tishri), in which the Day of Atonement and *Sukkoth* in any case occurred.[13] The importance of the seventh month was marked by increased sacrifice. Now, however, the rabbis also insist that, while Nisan is the new year for kings and festivals, Tishri is the new year for agricultural years and sabbatical years and Jubilees (Mishnah *Rosh Hashanah* 1:1). In so doing, they marked their triumph over the Essenes and other enthusiasts for a strictly solar calendar.

Pentecost/*Shavuoth* (Weeks)

Seven weeks after the close of the entire festival of Passover and Unleavened Bread came the feast called Weeks or Pentecost (in Greek, referring to the period of fifty days that was involved; see Leviticus 23:15–22 and Deuteronomy 16:9–12).[14] The waving of the sheaf before the Lord at the close of Passover anticipated the

---

[13] See Leviticus 23:24, Numbers 29:1, and the discussion in Abraham P. Bloch, *The Biblical and Historical Background of the Jewish Holy Days* (New York: Ktav, 1978), 13–25. He points out (p. 14) that the use of the trumpet on festal occasions during the biblical period (see Numbers 10:10) means there was nothing unique about sounding the shofar on what was later called *Rosh Hashanah*. As he notes (p. 17), the insistence of Rabbi Yochanan ben Zakkai after 70 C.E. that the shofar be blown within the synagogue (see Babylonian Talmud, *Rosh Hashanah* 29b; cf. 33b, in regard to Gamaliel, who also seems to have named the feast, 15a) marks a signal moment in the emergence of rabbinic Judaism. For that reason, we should note that the contributions of Yochanan and Gamaliel are already indicated in the Mishnah (*Rosh Hashanah* 4:1, 9), so that the festival seems clearly to have been shaped by the close of the second century C.E.

[14] As Schauss has shown (*The Jewish Festivals*, 87–88), because Leviticus 23:15–16 refers to counting from the day after the Sabbath, deviations in timing

greater harvest (especially of wheat; see Exodus 34:22) which was to follow in the summer, and that is just what Weeks celebrates (so Leviticus 23:10–15).

An especially interesting feature of the range of sacrifices involved in the celebration of Weeks is the specific mention of *leavened* bread (Leviticus 23:17). Every major festival occasions a large expenditure of celebratory wealth, but why should mention be made of yeast here, which has been so rigorously removed some seven weeks before? That reference enables us to see two features of both Unleavened Bread and Weeks which might otherwise have escaped us.

First, the removal of leaven early in the spring is symmetrical with its reintroduction early in the summer; taken together, these festal practices make it clear that the removal of yeast was not intended to be definitive but contributes to Israel's usage of yeast through the year. Second (and relatedly), the bread which is specified as leavened is for human consumption. Although the context in which it is presented is sacrificial, this bread is not for divine consumption; it is for waving before God, not for assigning to him in the fire. For that reason, the fact of its being leavened does not abrogate the general requirement that cereal given to God should be unleavened. One of the major points of sacrifice generally is that Israel enjoys what is assigned to Israel and that God takes pleasure in what is God's; together, Unleavened Bread and Weeks show us that yeast was Israel's and the appropriate celebration of the festivals would assure the continuation of that benefit.

The agricultural focus of Weeks was so emphatic that—as is often noted—no precise connection is made within the Bible between that festival and the formation of Israel in a way comparable with Passover and Unleavened Bread. Still, the book of Deuteronomy makes the association between Weeks and remembering that one was a slave in Egypt: this remembrance, in turn, motivated one to observe and perform the statutes (Deuteronomy 16:12). By the time of the book of *Jubilees* in the second century B.C.E., the

---

were inevitable. Does Sabbath here mean the day of the feast or the Sabbath after the feast? If the former, which day of the feast would be at issue? Differing answers would give you Weeks on 6 Sivan (as in dominant Pharisaic and Orthodox circles), or always on a Sunday (as among the Samaritans and Karaites, following the Sadducees, according to Schauss), or on 12 Sivan (as among the Falashas) or even on 15 Sivan (as in the book of *Jubilees*). James VanderKam follows this line of reasoning and shows that the dating of *Jubilees* was also followed in the *Temple Scroll* of Qumran; see "Weeks, Festival of," *Anchor Bible Dictionary*, 6:895–97.

feast is associated with the covenant and the Torah as mediated by Moses (see *Jubilees* 1:1–26), as well as with the covenants with Noah (*Jubilees* 6:1, 10–11, 17–19) and Abraham (*Jubilees* 15:1–16). The covenantal association is perhaps already evident in Deuteronomy 26:1–11, in the offering of first fruits, which may have occurred at the time of Pentecost (see Exodus 34:22; Numbers 28:26). At a later stage, certain rabbinic traditions (but by no means all) would make the giving of the law in Exodus 19 the lectionary reading of Weeks (see *Megillah* 31a in the Babylonian Talmud, departing from Exodus 19:1), and would recall that the word of God was split into the seventy languages of the nations (Babylonian Talmud *Shabbath* 88b). Although the specific association with the giving of the Torah cannot be established as a controlling sense by the time of the New Testament, that meaning grew out of the generative connection between Weeks and divine covenant which had been made long before.

Tabernacles/*Sukkoth* (Huts)

The last great harvest, and the last of the three great festivals, is *Sukkoth,* meaning Tabernacles (tents) or Booths (huts). Actually, the term *sukkah* can also mean "thicket," such as an animal might lurk in: the point is to refer to a rough, natural shelter of plaited branches which would permit the celebrants to lodge in the fields. Grapes and olives were taken in at this time; they required particular care in handling and storage, and sometimes it was prudent to remain near enough to protect the ripened yield. Camping in the fields was a wise practice. *Sukkoth,* in its material and social dimensions, was a feast of particular joy and the principal festival of ancient Israel (and may indeed pre-date Israel; see Judges 9:27). It could simply be referred to as "Feast of the LORD," without further specification (see Leviticus 23:39; Judges 21:19), in view of its prominence.

As in the cases of Passover and of Weeks, the festival was also associated with the formation of Israel, and the *sukkoth* were held to be reminiscent of the people's period in the wilderness. But that was a later development, reflected from the time of the Priestly source (see Leviticus 23:39–43), which also specified the greatest amount of sacrifice for *Sukkoth* among all the festivals (see Numbers 29). Deuteronomy also would regard the three great festivals—Passover, Weeks, and *Sukkoth*—as feasts of pilgrimage (Deuteronomy

16:16–17) involving travel to the central sanctuary in Jerusalem, although they were in origin (and probably remained in practice, under various forms) local, festal celebrations.

The success of the Deuteronomic calendar corresponds to the emergence of the canon and results in the agricultural year becoming the covenantal year: the cycle of exodus, Sinai, and wilderness was superimposed on the cycle of barley, wheat, and grapes. The temple (the only place where sacrifice could be offered) became the focus of all three festivals. But it is noteworthy that of the three major feasts of Judaism, *Sukkoth* has survived best in the rabbinic revision of practice following the destruction of the temple. Sacrifice, of course, is not involved, but the construction of the *sukkah* and associated practices of festivity make this the most joyous occasion of the Jewish year (see the mishnaic tractate *Sukkah*).

Yet in ancient Israel, whether the focus is on the agricultural or the covenantal explanation, sacrifice was central to all the festivals, and sacrifice on a monumental scale. It is not surprising that *Sukkoth* is marked as the greatest sacrifice in terms of the quantity and value of offerings, because it came at the time of year when the disposable wealth of produce was at its height. The underlying dynamic of sacrifice is that when Israel enjoys the produce of God's land with God, according to the preparation and timing and consumption God desires, Israel is blessed. Sacrifice is a holy consumption which carries in itself the promise of further enjoyment. Penance may of course be involved in sacrifice, but most of the sacrifices of Israel—the festival sacrifices above all—are emphatically understood as occasions of communal, festal joy such as "developed" societies in our time find difficult to come by. The temple was a place of dedicated rejoicing. In this context, it is vital to note that, even before it was linked with the period in the wilderness, *Sukkoth* was associated with the time Solomon dedicated the temple (see 1 Kings 8:2). The temple itself is a house of joy, and its dedication is crucial.

Tishri (during which *Sukkoth* occurs) is the seventh month, and the temple's dedication then made *Sukkoth* the time when, in a sabbath year, the Torah would be read out (so Deuteronomy 31:9–13). That is the basis of the later rabbinic celebration of *Simchat Torah* ("joy of the law"), which closes *Sukkoth*. The number seven, of course, is basic to the entire calendar which coordinates the feasts, each of which was to last a week. (Although this is not specified in the case of Weeks, both its status as a festal convocation [Leviticus

23:21] and its name make it probable.) The weeks of the year mark
out the quarters of the lunar month, and each week ends with the
Sabbath, which is itself a regular feast. (The timing of each major
feast in the middle of its month corresponds to the full moon, as is
appropriate for a feast of harvest.) The sabbath year and the Jubilee
year (the sabbath of sabbaths) fit into the scheme which makes
seven a basic unit of measurement. So there is a sense in which
Tishri marks the new year, as well as the month Abib (see Exodus
12:2; 13:4, later called Nisan), the month of the Passover. When
the book of Zechariah envisages the establishment of worship for
all the nations in Jerusalem in a new, eschatological dispensation, it
is natural that the feast concerned should be *Sukkoth* (Zechariah
14:16–21).

Chanukkah and other festivals

During the Maccabean period, the restoration of worship in the
temple was accomplished in the ninth month, and the feast which
marks this occasion was known as the Dedication, *Chanukkah* (see
1 Maccabees 4:36–61). That seems to have been a popular feast as
well as an officially sanctioned festival, but not as important as
Purim, a spring festival one month before Passover. *Purim* celebrated victory over people such as the legendary Haman, described
as "the Jews' harasser" (Esther 8:1); the book of Esther was read
dramatically and with the enthusiastic participation of the audience. The term *Purim* (meaning dice or "lots," Esther 3:7) itself derives from Babylonian religion, which appears to have provided
much of the practice and myth of the feast; there was a strong tendency during the Maccabean period to call it the Day of Mordecai,
naming it after Esther's uncle, and to assimilate it to the Day of
Nicanor, the commemoration of a military triumph (see 2 Maccabees 14:12–15:36).

The initial dedication of the temple (and of the system of the sabbatical cycle) at *Sukkoth* makes it quite understandable that the
principal occasion of repentance, the Day of Atonement, takes
place just prior to *Sukkoth* (see Leviticus 16). As in the case of other
occasions of penitence, the sacrifice takes a distinct form: what was
usually consumed by people alongside God's consumption is now
offered to God alone. But the national range of the Day of Atonement makes this occasion uniquely important as an act of rededi-
catory penitence.

After the destruction of Solomon's temple, fasts became conventional during the fourth, fifth, seventh, and tenth months (see Zechariah 8:19). It seems reasonable to associate them with 17 Tammuz, 9 Av, 3 Tishri, and 10 Tebet in rabbinic practice.[15]

All these are related to the stages of the destruction of the temple in rabbinic literature, however, and consensus has it that fasting prior to the arson of Titus was more intimately associated with penitential prayer than with the recollection of historical calamities (see Esther 4:1–3, 15–16; Judith 4:9–15).[16]

The annulment of these fasts is predicted in the book of Zechariah, on the grounds that the final, eschatological *Sukkoth* will swallow up all commemorations of defeat and the need for penitence in its ultimate joy. But fasting seems to have become an increasingly important aspect of Judaic practice, and it is interesting that what one gives of oneself in penitence (flesh and blood) can be compared with what earlier had been offered on the altar in rabbinic literature (see Babylonian Talmud *Berakhoth* 17a).

---

[15] See Ismar Elbogen, *Der jüdische Gottesdienst in seiner geschichtlichen Entwicklung* (Hildesheim: Olms, 1967), 126–30.

[16] See Jacob Milgrom, Moshe David Herr, and Cecil Roth, "Fasting, and Fast Days," *Encyclopedia Judaica*, 6:1189–96.

CHAPTER FOUR

Festal Christianity

The New Testament does not present a complete calendar of festivals and holy days, nor does it explain its own view of time. Attempts to portray the Gospels as lectionaries that follow the calendar of Judaism are notable for their complexity, but none of them has been widely accepted (as we have seen in Chapter Two). Indeed, part of Christianity's problem with time, I shall argue in the conclusion, is that the rhythm and interval that provide the experience of time with coherence and meaning are *deliberately* excised from the Gospels' presentation. They speak within the calendar of Judaism and therefore refer to principal feasts, but not within a systematic treatment of time. The Gospels are located inside time, but their concerns are not temporal.

The Gospels self-consciously speak *sub specie aeternitatis*, under the aspect of eternity. They are focused on a particular act of *mimesis*, the imitation of Christ, and they consider that *mimesis* to be outside the realm of time, for reasons we will discuss in the next chapter. So the Gospels offer no easy advice for how to understand time or festival; much less do they set out the feasts of Judaism systematically. In this regard, as in many others, the New Testament frustrates the interests of conventional history.

Nonetheless a deep engagement with the calendar of Judaism is reflected in the Gospels. The calendar of Judaism frequently provides the setting of crucial events and teachings. Feasts are sometimes explicitly named, and their significance often turns out to be of pivotal importance for understanding the narrative or appreciating Jesus' teaching. At other times, the largely atemporal presentation of the Gospels results in their making no mention of the festal contexts involved, but these contexts are nonetheless evident in what Jesus says and does.

Whether the festal contexts are explicit or implicit, none of the cases we will treat here can be regarded as incidental. A feast or a fast is by definition—and in the observance of communities—a moment when the identity of a people is expressed. Jesus' followers, whether in Galilee or Jerusalem, were imbued with Israel's holy calendar, and after the resurrection feasts were no less important to the disciples who gathered around leaders such as Peter and James. In fact, feasts permit us to trace the evolution of Jesus' movement: during his own life, under the leadership of Peter and James, and then as it moved into the distinct literary forms which brought us the Gospels a generation after Jesus' death.

The texts of the Gospels as we can presently read them were products of the interactions among these various groups. Sources within the Gospels can be discerned in the way different leaders are named, in variations of subject and setting and style as one reads from passage to passage, and in evidence of tension between one passage and another. These are standard ways of inferring when we are dealing with the contribution of one circle of usage (for example, centered around James) rather than another (centered around Peter, for instance). Each Gospel shows us how such sources were brought together within major church centers during the first century.

Inferences in regard to sources are not just data. Despite the certainty some scholars attribute to the existence of the famous "Q" source, for example, no one has ever discovered a copy from antiquity. Because sources are explanations of the evidence at hand, there is necessarily an element of uncertainty in identifying a given circle of usage. But it is misleading to pretend each Gospel was written by a single author: the meaning of our texts can only be approached within the context of the primitive Christian circles that produced the Gospels. In this task, the festivals of Judaism are extremely helpful, since the distinctive concerns of Jesus, Peter, and James seem to have crystallized around the major feasts of the temple (*Sukkoth*, Pentecost, and Passover respectively). Once those festal cycles have been discerned, the identification of further constellations of material around feasts is also possible.

The most distinctive appropriation of a Judaic festival within the church was occasioned by Passover. Although the Gospel according to John presents Jesus' death at the time the paschal lambs were slain (John 19:14, 31), the Synoptics portray the Last Supper as a Seder, the meal of Passover (Matthew 26:17–29; Mark 14:12–16; Luke 22:7–13). There are several reasons for which this identification is implausible.[1] No mention is made in the account of the supper of the lamb (much less its selection and preparation days before), the bitter herbs, the unleavened bread, or the exodus from Egypt, all of which are formally prescribed in the book of Exodus (chapter 12). Moreover, the cultic authorities are presented as solemnly deciding to act in the case of Jesus *before* the feast itself (Matthew 26:3–5; Mark 14:1–2). It seems clear that Jesus died near the time of Passover (having entered Jerusalem at or near *Sukkoth,* as we shall see), and that this timing then became coordinated with the Passover itself within the practice of the church.

The attempt to cram all the events leading up to his death into a single "Holy Week" is implausible as history, as is the thesis (which some scholars have derived from the Synoptics) that Jesus' public activity lasted only one year, culminating in this final Passover. The liturgical power of this feast—which became the principal festival of Christianity, even while the temple still stood and *Sukkoth* was the principal festival of Judaism—will have to be explained as we analyze the different circles of influence and practice. But as matters stand for the moment, we need simply to avoid being dazzled by the impression, frequently drawn from a hasty reading of the Synoptic Gospels, that Passover was the only feast that mattered greatly to Jews or Christians. The dominance of Passover in the New Testament is primarily a function of how the Pascha (as Christians called the Passover in Greek, reflecting the Aramaic pronunciation) emerged as the main Christian feast. This dominance can only be explained by means of sensitivity to the practices of the primitive Church and how these practices influenced the development of the Gospels.

The Tabernacles of Jesus

Jesus' entry into Jerusalem, as we have noticed, is likely to have occurred well before the time of his death in the spring prior to Passover. His procession at or near the time of *Sukkoth* would

---

[1] For the development of the Eucharist and the texts that relate to it, see Chilton, *A Feast of Meanings: Eucharistic Theologies from Jesus through Johannine Circles* (Supplements to Novum Testamentum 72; Leiden: Brill, 1994).

help to explain the text of the Gospels. Leafy branches featured centrally in the procession of *Sukkoth;* the Mishnah calls the bundle of myrtle, willow, and palm, which was waved about with lemons, a *"lulab"* (see Mishnah *Sukkah* 3:1–4:5 and the related provision for the booths in Nehemiah 8:14–16). These bundles of abundance are a key symbol within the Gospel scene (see Matthew 21:8; Mark 11:8; and John 12:13). In the cry "Hosanna" (meaning, "save us"; see Matthew 21:9; Mark 11:9; John 12:13) a characteristic element of the *Sukkoth* celebration also comes to expression (see *Sukkah* 3:9; 4:5).

Procession to the temple with *lulab*s in hand was a requirement of this feast, even on the Sabbath, because it was an intrinsic part of the festivity (*Sukkah* 4:4). There was a vigorous, sometimes even violent strain in all this. The same passage of the Mishnah relates that attendants used to scatter *lulab*s for people to collect, but this led to people fighting over them and even hitting one another with *lulab*s, so that practice was stopped. The problem will be familiar to anyone who has tried to keep order in a Sunday school on Palm Sunday. Although my congregants can find that a nuisance, I have long enjoyed this rambunctious affinity with the genuine setting of Jesus' entry into Jerusalem.

When Simon Maccabeus entered Jerusalem, he enjoyed a similar triumph (see 1 Maccabees 13:51), so it is clear that the tenor of *Sukkoth* was not limited to the feast itself. But Jesus' entry is marked as a religious occasion, not only by the cries of "Hosanna," but by the usage of material from the Hallel, a group of psalms (Psalms 113–118) sung all through *Sukkoth*. Psalm 118:25–26 is actually cited as the crowd's song in Matthew 21:9, Mark 11:9, Luke 19:38, and John 12:13, and it is specified in the Mishnah as a portion of the Hallel to be sung (see *Sukkah* 4:5). In his commentary on Mark's Gospel, William L. Lane wrote that the "strongest argument for a Tabernacles setting for the entry into Jerusalem is found in the reference to the branches of greenery in connection with the use of 'Hosanna'."[2]

Although a strong argument, the connections between Jesus' entry and *Sukkoth* are in fact deeper. They become evident when we consider the formative impact of the book of Zechariah on the

---

[2] William L. Lane, *The Gospel according to Mark* (London: Marshall, Morgan & Scott, 1974), 397 n. 17. The theory of a *Sukkoth* timing has been widely discussed since the article of T. W. Manson, "The Cleansing of the Temple," *Bulletin of the John Rylands Library* 33 (1951): 271–82.

Gospels' accounts, because Zechariah focused on the feast of *Sukkoth*. The Targum (Aramaic version) of the last chapter of the prophecy predicts that God's kingdom will be manifested over the entire earth when the offerings of *Sukkoth* are presented by both Israelites and non-Jews at the temple. It further predicts that these worshipers will prepare and offer their sacrifices themselves, without the intervention of middle men. The last words of the book promise that "there shall never again be a *trader* in the *sanctuary* of the Lord of hosts at that *time*" (*Targum Zechariah* 14:21).[3] The thrust of the targumic prophecy motivated Jesus in the dramatic confrontation he provoked in the temple.

The Targum emphasized the coming transformation of worship in the temple as well as the ultimate vindication of Israel, which would give the people of God back their land. Jesus himself had been pushed out of Galilee by Antipas (see Luke 13:31–33), just as the Israelites had been displaced from their control of their own territory by the Romans. Zechariah's vision of a *Sukkoth* that restored the land to Israel and the temple to the sacrifice God desired was a fundamental aspect of Jesus' purpose during his last weeks in Jerusalem. The Romans would be banished and Zion's gates opened to all who would join with Israel there in worship (*Targum Zechariah* 14:9): "*And the Kingdom of the* LORD *shall be revealed* upon all *the inhabitants of* the earth; at that *time they shall serve before the* LORD *with one accord, for* his name *is established in the world; there is none apart from him.*"

The Targum not only specifies that Zechariah's vision is of the kingdom, it also spells out, in a way the Hebrew text does not, the immediate impact of that kingdom upon *all* of humanity. Peter had built huts or *sukkoth* on Mount Hermon for the Transfiguration (Matthew 16:28–17:8; Mark 9:1–8; Luke 9:27–36), so as to realize and memorialize the vision of Jesus and Moses and Elijah dwelling on earth, among the disciples of Jesus.[4] Zechariah prophesied

---

[3] In order to indicate where a Targum innovates in comparison with the underlying Hebrew text, it has become conventional to use italics. In this case, the prophecy against trade in the temple becomes stronger in the Aramaic version. For a translation of the Aramaic Targum, see Kevin J. Cathcart and Robert P. Gordon, *The Targum of the Minor Prophets* (The Aramaic Bible 14; Wilmington: Glazier, 1989).

[4] I have described in detail the *Sukkoth* connection of the Transfiguration in an academic essay, "The Transfiguration: Dominical Assurance and Apostolic Vision," *New Testament Studies* 27 (1980): 115–24 and in narrative terms, *Rabbi Jesus*, 174–96.

that at the feast of *Sukkoth* the temple would become the definitive tabernacle—the place where Israel would be regenerated and the visionary world Peter glimpsed on the mountain would take on flesh and blood. Sacrifice in the temple would become a universal feast with God, open to all peoples who accepted the truth initially to be revealed in Israel alone.

The focus of Jesus' action on the temple, in his occupation of the outer court as a protest and enactment of the kind of purity he demanded there (Matthew 21:12–13; Mark 11:15–17; Luke 19:45–46; John 2:14–17), comports well with the pivotal place of the temple at the close of the book of Zechariah.[5] Even Jesus' appropriation of property—the foal which he rides into the city (Matthew 21:1–7; Mark 11:1–7; Luke 19:29–35)—is an enactment of Zechariah's prophecy. The book itself claims that the very horses in Jerusalem will be marked ornamentally with the words "holy to the LORD" (Zechariah 14:20), and Zechariah 9:9 presents the messianic king as riding on a colt. For a royal figure, garments might well be strewn in the way (2 Kings 9:12). That was all the more natural at *Sukkoth* in the case of Jesus, who was a son of David (see Matthew 21:7–9; Mark 11:7–10; Luke 19:35–38).

At the time of *Sukkoth*, worn priestly garments were turned into wicks for illumination, and flaming torches accompanied the song and dance of the procession (Mishnah *Sukkah* 5:3–4). What were a few more garments tossed about in such a mêlée? All this festivity was appropriate because this messiah made known the identity of the Lord as king, and in the Targum—as in Jesus' preaching and his followers' acclamation—that revelation is called the kingdom of God (*Targum Zechariah* 14:9; see Mark 11:10; Luke 19:38; John 12:13). In all of this, the deep connection of Jesus' orientation to an eschatological understanding of *Sukkoth* as exemplified in the book of Zechariah is evident.

The Pentecost of Peter

For those Christians who recollected the twelve gathered around Peter in Jerusalem, the timing of the coming of the Holy Spirit was unequivocal (Acts 2:1–4). That memory gave "Pentecost" a meaning within Christianity—as the moment of spiritual endowment—which in the popular mind has nothing to do with Judaism. The

---

[5] See Chilton, "Jesus' Occupation of the Temple," *The Temple of Jesus*, 91–111, and "The Sacrificial Program of Jesus," *The Temple of Jesus*, 113–36.

debate regarding how literally this story should be taken has been as brisk as it has been perennial. The present concern is not with the experience behind the text, but how the text was remembered with a Pentecostal meaning that is fully consistent with ancient Judaic practice and theology.

The stress that the full number of the twelve (Matthias having replaced Judas; Acts 1:15–26) were together in a single place emphasizes that the gift of the Spirit pertains to Israel. Precisely at Pentecost, the Spirit is portrayed as descending on the twelve apostles, and they speak God's praises in the various languages of those assembled from the four points of the compass for that summer feast of harvest, both Jews and proselytes (Acts 2:5–12). The mention of proselytes (2:10) and the emphasis that those gathered came from "every nation under heaven" (2:5) clearly point ahead to the inclusion of non-Jews by means of baptism within Acts.[6]

But even Peter's explanation of the descent of the Spirit alludes to this inclusion (Acts 2:14–37). He quotes from the prophet Joel (2:28–32 in the Septuagint): "And it will be in the last days, says God, that I will pour out from my Spirit upon all flesh."[7] "All flesh," not only historic Israel, is to receive of God's Spirit (Acts 2:37–42); the twelve are its focus of radiation, not its limit, and Acts speaks of the baptism of some three thousand people in response to Peter's invitation (Acts 2:41).

The outward radiance of the Spirit makes Pentecost the most notable feast (in calendrical and theological terms) of Peter and his circle. The distinctively Christian take on Pentecost is easily described on the basis of the New Testament. What is less clear is how that theology developed from Judaic *Shavuoth*. Still, it is worth specifying this Petrine theology as it has been taken up within Christianity before trying to explain it. When Peter spoke in the house of Cornelius in Acts 10, the Spirit fell upon those who were listening, and those there with Peter who were circumcised were astounded "that the gift of the Holy Spirit has been poured out even upon the

---

[6] So C. K. Barrett, *The Acts of the Apostles I* (The International Critical Commentary; Edinburgh: Clark, 1994), 108. See also Lars Hartman, *"Into the Name of the Lord Jesus": Baptism in the Early Church* (Studies of the New Testament and Its World; Edinburgh: Clark, 1997), 131–33. Hartman observes the coherence with Luke 24:44–49, which shows, together with the preaching attributed to Peter in the house of Cornelius, that from an early stage the narrative of Jesus' passion was connected with the catechesis leading to baptism.

[7] Barrett, *Acts of the Apostles*, 129–57, presents a fine analysis on how the text of Joel deeply influenced the speech of Peter as a whole.

nations" (10:44–45). The choice of the verb "to pour out" is no co-incidence: it resonates with the quotation of Joel in Acts 2:17.

Indeed, those in Cornelius's house praise God "in tongues" (10:46) in a manner reminiscent of the apostles' prophecy at Pentecost. (The assumption here and in Acts 2 is that the Spirit makes people more articulate than they normally are. That is also the way Paul believes tongues are properly to be conceived, as opposed to those who see the gift of tongues as resulting in incoherence [see 1 Corinthians 14].) Peter directs that this non-Jewish household be baptized "in the name of Christ Jesus" (10:47–48).

That is just the direction Peter gave earlier to his sympathetic hearers at Pentecost (2:37–38). Probably in the case of his speech at Pentecost, and more definitely in the case of his speech in the house of Cornelius, Peter's directions were in Greek, and we should understand that immersion is not for the purpose of purification, as in Judaic practice (including John the Baptist's); it is into *Jesus' name,* which has entered the Greek language *(Iesous)* as defining the aim of baptism. Christian baptism, immersion into the name of Jesus with reception of the Holy Spirit, was developed within the practice of the circle of Peter.

Taken together, the two passages do not suggest any real dispute as to whether the gift of the Spirit followed or preceded baptism into Jesus' name. The point is rather that belief in and baptism into him is connected directly with the outpouring of God's Spirit. The apparent disruption of the usual model in Acts 10 is intended to call attention to the artificiality (from the point of view of the emergent Petrine theology) of attempting to withhold baptism from those who believe (as Peter actually says in 10:47).[8]

Still, two questions immediately arise at this point. First, why would it have been natural for Peter to have extended baptism to non-Jews on the basis of the outpouring of the Spirit, when he was still sensitive to the scruples of Judaism? (And that sensitivity is recorded by Paul, a contemporary witness [see Galatians 2:11–14].[9]) Second, where did Peter understand the new infusion of the Spirit to have derived from?

Those two questions have a single answer. The source of the Spirit is Jesus as raised from the dead. In Peter's speech at Pente-

---

[8] See Hartman, *"Into the Name of the Lord Jesus,"* 133–36.
[9] For a discussion, see Chilton and Neusner, *Judaism in the New Testament,* 99–104, 108–11.

cost, Jesus, having been exalted to the right hand of God, receives the promise of the Holy Spirit from the Father and pours it out on his followers (2:33). The Spirit that is poured out, then, comes directly from the majesty of God, from his rule over creation as a whole. This is the Spirit as it hovered over the waters at the beginning of creation (Genesis 1:2) and not as limited to Israel. Because the Spirit is of God, who creates people in the divine image, its presence marks God's own activity, in which all those who follow Jesus are to be included.

Jesus' own program had involved realizing God's kingdom on the authority of his possession of God's Spirit (see Matthew 12:28). Now, as a consequence of the resurrection, Jesus had poured out that same Spirit upon those who would follow him. Baptism in the Spirit (see Acts 1:4–5) and baptism into the name of Jesus were one and the same for that reason. That was why, as Lars Hartman suggests, believing that Jesus was God's Son and calling upon his name were the occasions on which the Spirit was to be received.[10] In the new environment of God's Spirit which the resurrection signaled, baptism was indeed, as Matthew 28:19 indicates, an activity and an experience which involved the Father (the source of one's identity), the Son (the agent of one's identity), and the Holy Spirit (the medium of one's identity).

The timing of Pentecost and the arrival of the Spirit were already implicitly linked within the festival calendar of Judaism. In the book of Exodus, it is in the third month, the month when *Shavuoth* came, that Moses ascended Sinai (Exodus 19:1–25). This association was so strong that during the rabbinic period Eleazar could laconically remark that Pentecost was "the day on which the Torah was given" (*Pesachim* 68b in the Babylonian Talmud). The image of all the people gathered at the base of Sinai in Exodus 19 may be reflected in the depiction of Jews (including proselytes) from every point of the compass gathering for Pentecost in Jerusalem (Acts 2:5–11). In the book of Exodus, the Spirit is associated with the mediation of the Torah and its provisions, especially where it concerns preparations for the priests and arrangements for the tabernacle (see Exodus 31:1–11; 35:30–35).

After Moses had received all of those commandments, the book of Numbers portrays Israel as setting out from the wilderness of Sinai on the twentieth day of the second month (Numbers

---

[10] Hartman, *"Into the Name of the Lord Jesus,"* 140, citing Acts 8:37; 22:16.

10:11–12). After an indeterminate time, but comfortably within range of the usual observation of Pentecost, the people are portrayed as provoking God to anger, so that fire breaks out in the camp (Numbers 11:1–3). Their complaints about provisions leads to Moses' choice of seventy elders, who receive God's Spirit with him at the tabernacle and prophesy (see Numbers 11:4–25). Two people left in the camp, Eldad and Medad, also prophesy, but this brings no objection from Moses. On the contrary, Moses would prefer that all God's people were prophets (Numbers 11:26–29).

The association in this passage of fire, Spirit, and prophecy makes for a stunning similarity with the scene in Acts, and the specification of seventy elders is also striking, since seventy is also the number of the nations in Judaism.[11] After all, although those specified as present in Jerusalem are said to be Jews and proselytes, the theme of Acts in its entirety turns on how apostolic prophecy radiates outward to the entire inhabited world.

The association of Weeks with the covenant with Noah (see *Jubilees* 6:1, 10–11, 17–19), the patriarch before the Israelite patriarchs, may help to explain why, in the minds of Peter's followers, the coming of the Spirit at Pentecost was to extend to humanity at large. Hellenistic Judaism seems especially to have cherished this association with Noah, because he was a paradigm of the righteous and wise non-Israelite. The Sibyl, for example—the premiere prophetess of Greco-Roman culture—is Noah's daughter-in-law in the *Sibylline Oracles* 3:823–827.

Kirsopp Lake called attention to the requirements made of Gentiles within the Fourth Book of the *Sibylline Oracles* (4:24–34):[12]

> Happy will be those of earthly men who will cherish the great God, blessing before eating, drinking and having confidence in piety. They will deny all temples and altars they see: purposeless transports of dumb stones, defiled by animates' blood and sacrifices of four-footed

---

[11] See Jöram Friberg, "Numbers and Counting," *Anchor Bible Dictionary* (ed. D. N. Freedman; New York; Doubleday, 1992), 4:1139–46.

[12] Kirsopp Lake, "The Apostolic Council of Jerusalem," *The Beginnings of Christianity* (ed. F. J. Foakes Jackson and Kirsopp Lake; 5 vols.; Grand Rapids: Baker, 1979), 5:195–212, 208–9, with a citation of the Greek text. For an English rendering and fine introductions and explanations, see John J. Collins, "Sibylline Oracles: A New Translation and Introduction," *The Old Testament Pseudepigrapha* (ed. J. H. Charlesworth; 2 vols.; Garden City, N.Y.: Doubleday, 1983), 1:317–472. Collins dates this work within the first century but after the eruption of Vesuvius in 79 C.E. (pp. 381–82). With due caution, he assigns Book Four a Syrian provenience.

animals. But they will behold the great renown of the one God, neither breaking into reckless murder, nor transacting what is stolen for gain, which are cold happenings. They do not have shameful desire for another's bed, nor hateful and repulsive abuse of a male.

What is especially striking about this prophecy is that it is directed to the people of Asia and Europe (*Sibylline Oracles* 4:1) through the mouth of the Sibyl (*Sibylline Oracles* 4:22–23), the legendary oracle of mantic counsel. Her utterance here is explicitly backed up by the threat of eschatological judgment for all (*Sibylline Oracles* 4:40–48).

Lake's comparison with the apostolic council in which Peter and James both took part (Acts 15:1–29) seems apposite. Of course, the Noachic theme cannot be limited to Peter or his circle in any strict sense; the point is rather that the Petrine theology found a deep resonance with the extension of Jesus' movement in a field prepared by Hellenistic Judaism.

A growing body of opinion has found that the emphasis upon prophecy in Luke-Acts accords with the perspectives of Hellenistic historians such as Diodorus Siculus and Dionysius of Halicarnassus.[13] The place of Sibylline prophecies, deriving from a prophetess whose origin "was already lost in the mist of legend by the fifth century" C.E.,[14] is prominent in both. But while Luke-Acts invokes the motif of prophecy (both literary and contemporary), the Sibyl makes no appearance in a work which is, after all, the longest in the New Testament.

This curious ambivalence, in which a major work of Christianity invokes themes of Hellenistic prophecy and yet refuses to associate itself with contemporary traditions, reflects a characteristic attitude of the movement. The way for a synthesis of Hellenistic oracles and Hebrew prophecy had been prepared by works such as the *Sibylline Oracles* of Hellenistic Judaism, but Luke-Acts insists upon the testimony to *Jesus'* name (directly or indirectly) as an indispensable criterion of true prophecy.[15] This two-volume work is cosmopolitan in its range from the outset (see Luke 1:1–4) and yet is also rooted particularly in Jesus as he reveals God's Spirit during

---

[13] See John T. Squires, *The Plan of God in Luke-Acts* (Society for New Testament Studies Monograph Series 76; Cambridge: Cambridge University Press, 1993), 121–54.

[14] See Collins, "Sibylline Oracles," 317.

[15] See Chilton and Jacob Neusner, *Types of Authority in Formative Judaism and Christianity* (London: Routledge, 1999), 116–19.

his life (see Luke 4:18) and after his resurrection (Acts 2:32–33). Two key aspects of Christianity in its primitive phase, an embrace of the possibility of prophecy and an insistence that Jesus alone is the source of Spirit, are grounded in a literally Pentecostal theology deriving from the circle of Peter.

We have seen that the development of ethical requirements for Gentiles in view of eschatological judgment was part of the ethos of Hellenistic Judaism at the time Luke-Acts was composed. The demands cited by Lake in the Fourth Book of the *Sibylline Oracles*[16] comport well with the requirements set out in Acts 15, except for the specific proscription of blood. (That, however, is featured prominently with Noah in *Jubilees* 6:10.) Still, reciting a blessing prior to eating might suggest that what is eaten is to be pure, and immersion is mentioned later in the *Sibylline Oracles* (4:165), so the issue is scarcely outside the range of concerns of Hellenistic Judaism.

That concern also is inherent in the Third Book of the *Sibylline Oracles*, which John J. Collins dates within the period 163–145 B.C.E.[17] The Sibyl is portrayed as Noah's daughter-in-law (*Sibylline Oracles* 3:823–827), and of course it was Noah whom God instructed with the commandment not to consume blood or to shed human blood (Genesis 9:4–6). Noah receives similar treatment in Books One and Two of the *Sibylline Oracles*.

The dates of Books One and Two of the corpus are uncertain and the Christian additions are evident, but Collins is on secure ground in his argument that the Judaic redaction was completed before 70 C.E. in Phrygia.[18] Noah is here made an articulate preacher of repentance to all peoples (*Sibylline Oracles* 1:128–129) in an elegant expansion of the biblical story (1:125–282) that describes the ark landing in Phrygia (1:262). The persistence of such an association between Noah and Asia Minor is reflected by 1 Peter 3:20, where the number of those in the ark (eight) is stressed, as in the *Sibylline Oracles* 1:281, in comparison with those who were punished.

Pentecostal imagery, however, was applied much more directly to the Spirit of God by Paul, a teacher known to have been influenced by Peter. The waving of the sheaf before the Lord at the close of Passover anticipated the greater harvest to follow in the summer,

---

[16] Lake also cites 4:162–70.
[17] Collins, "Sibylline Oracles," 355.
[18] Collins, "Sibylline Oracles," 331.

and that is just what Weeks celebrates (so Leviticus 23:9–22). So the first fruits of Passover promised the more plentiful and diverse first fruits gathered and offered at Weeks (see Numbers 28:26–31). The language of first fruits is used metaphorically in Paul's theology to express the gift of the Spirit and resurrection (Romans 8:23; 11:16; 1 Corinthians 15:20, 23). We should expect to hear such connections with the Pentecostal theology of Peter in Paul's preaching, since he was one of Peter's students (Galatians 1:18). Likewise, it is predicatable that Paul was especially concerned with keeping the feast of Pentecost (see 1 Corinthians 16:8; Acts 20:16). That concern might seem to contradict what Paul said about other calendrical observations in his Letter to the Galatians (see Galatians 4:9–10; cf. 2:14). His commitment to the theology and even the calendar of Pentecost is an indication of the deep influence of Petrine theology upon him, and the penetration of its principal elements within the Hellenistic Church.

The keeping of Pentecost even correlates with the primordially Christian observation of Sunday as a day of gathering in Jesus' name. That custom of meeting on what quickly came to be called the Lord's Day corresponds to the timing of the resurrection of Jesus, of course, but also to priestly teaching concerning the celebration of Pentecost in the temple. This is revealed in a passage of Talmud whose violent language seems humorous, although it reflects a depth of theological animus (*Menachoth* 65a–b):[19]

> For the Boethusians say, The festival of Pentecost must always coincide with a Sunday [seven full weeks after the offering of the first sheaf of barley-grain, which in their view was offered only on a Sunday]. Rabban Yohanan ben Zakkai engaged with them and said to them, "You total and complete schmucks! How do you know it?" Not a single one of them could answer, except a doddering old fool, who stumbled and mumbled against him, saying, "Our lord, Moses, loved Israel and knew that Pentecost lasted for only one day, so he therefore made sure to place it on a Sunday, so that Israel would have a two day vacation." He recited in his regard the following verse: "It is an eleven day journey from Horeb to Kadesh Barnea by way of Mount Seir"

---

[19] This idiomatic translation and its explanatory insertions (in square brackets) are Jacob Neusner's in *The Talmud of Babylonia: An Academic Commentary. Vol. 29, Menahoth* (South Florida Academic Commentary Series 23; Atlanta: Scholars Press, 1996). The term "schmuck" is usually rendered "fool," and the Talmud refers to "the day after the Sabbath," rather than to "Sunday," but this remains a most vivid and apt translation. Cf. *Menachoth min Talmud Bavli* (Jerusalem: Vagshal, 1980).

(Deuteronomy 1:2). "Now if our lord, Moses, really loved Israel all that much, why did he delay them in the wilderness for forty years!" He said to him, "My lord, do you think you can get rid of me with that kind of garbage?" He said to him, "You total schmuck! Are you going to treat the complete Torah that is ours like the idle nattering and chattering that is all you can throw up? One verse of Scripture says, 'You shall count for yourself fifty days' (Leviticus 23:16), and another verse states, 'Seven weeks shall be complete' (Leviticus 23:15). So how about that? The one verse refers to a case in which the festival day coincides with the Sabbath, the other, when a festival day coincides with a week day. [Pentecost may coincide with any day of the week.]"

One plausible reason for Yohanan ben Zakkai's vehemence over this issue in the period after 70 C.E. (when he came to prominence) is that Sunday was being appropriated by a group of Pentecostal *minim* (heretics or sectarians), those who were faithful to the teachings of Peter's circle. For in this circle, as we will now go on to see, a Judaic theology was being framed which could compete with Yohanan's in the claim that it could survive the destruction of the temple.

In his analysis of baptism in the New Testament, Lars Hartman has observed that the phrase "into the name of" is not idiomatic Greek, but more probably reflects the Aramaic *leshun* (or Hebrew *leshem*). He adduces a passage from the Mishnah (*Zevachim* 4:6) in order to explain the meaning of the phrase.[20] There, the phrase clearly refers to those "for the sake of" whom a given sacrifice is offered.[21] Having understood that the generative meaning of the phrase is cultic, Hartman explains the significance of baptism in terms of the new community that is called into being:

> Here the people of the new covenant were gathered, cleansed, forgiven, sanctified and equipped with a new spirit. Indeed, the gathering itself can also be regarded as occurring "into the name of the Lord Jesus."[22]

Such an emphasis on the role of God's Spirit in baptism is fundamental from the point of view of the New Testament itself, as we have seen. Whether the formulation is of immersion "into" or "in"

---

[20] Hartman, *"Into the Name of the Lord Jesus,"* 37–50.

[21] That is precisely the translation in Jacob Neusner, *The Mishnah: A New Translation* (New Haven: Yale University Press, 1988), 707. See also *Pesachim* 60a, cited by Hartman on p. 49 n. 53.

[22] Hartman, *"Into the Name of the Lord Jesus,"* 47.

Jesus' name, the latter simply being better Greek, in either case Jesus is the occasion and place where the Spirit is encountered. Still, Hartman's study leaves open the question of why a phrase of cultic origin should have been used in connection with baptism.

Now we can see why it was natural within the Petrine circle to speak of immersion "into the name of Jesus": the cultic language was inspired by the environment of Pentecost. Those who entered into a fresh relationship to God by means of the Holy Spirit were themselves a kind of "first fruits," because they found their identity in relation to Christ or the Spirit as "first fruit" (so Romans 8:23; 11:16; 16:5; 1 Corinthians 15:20, 23; 16:15; James 1:18; Revelation 14:4). The wide range of that usage—a testimony to the influence of this Petrine theology—reflects the deeply Pentecostal character of primitive Christianity. Access to the covenant by means of the Spirit meant that believers entered sacrificially "into the name" *(eis to onoma)* of Jesus in baptism. Also within the Petrine circle, Eucharist was celebrated in covenantal terms, when one broke bread and shared the cup "into the remembrance of" *(eis ten anamnesin)* Jesus, a phrase associated with covenantal sacrifice (see Exodus 24:8).[23] Both baptism and Eucharist are sacrificial in the Petrine understanding, and both intimately involve the Spirit of God.

Hartman makes a similar point in regard to the continuing presence of the Spirit in his discussion of a famous passage from Paul (1 Corinthians 12:12–13):

> For just as the body is one and has many members, but all the members of the body, being many, are one body, so is Christ. Because by one Spirit we were all immersed into one body, whether Jews or Greeks, whether slaves or free, and we were all made to drink one Spirit.

As Hartman observes:

> The last clause of the verse, "We were all made to drink of one Spirit," could as well be translated "We all had the one Spirit poured over us." The Spirit not only brought the baptised persons into the body of Christ, but also remains with them as a divine active presence.[24]

The Spirit is understood to be the continuing medium of faithful existence in Christ, and for that reason it is as natural to associate it

---

[23] See Chilton, *A Feast of Meanings*, 75–92. Hartman, *"Into the Name of the Lord Jesus,"* 61, also approaches this idea.

[24] Hartman, *"Into the Name of the Lord Jesus,"* 67–68.

with Eucharist as with baptism. After all, Paul could also say that believers, like the Israelites, drank the same spiritual drink, which came from Christ (1 Corinthians 10:4),[25] and that the Israelites went through their own immersion (1 Corinthians 10:2).

Because the Spirit in question is God's and Jesus' at one and the same time, the range of its results is extremely broad. It is as manifest as God's own creativity, and as personal as an individual believer's conviction. Charles Gore skillfully brought that out in a study that still merits careful consideration:[26]

> It is true that St. Luke lays stress on the wonderful signs which marked the sudden arrival of the Spirit on, or just before, the day of Pentecost, and on the similar signs which marked the first bestowal of the gift upon the Gentiles, Cornelius and his companions, and again on the twelve men who had been disciples of John the Baptist and were now led on into the faith of Christ.[27] And he delights to recount the miracles of healing wrought by the apostles. But also courage in speaking the word, and wisdom, and faith, and large-hearted goodness are associated with the Spirit's presence,[28] and He is recognized not only as the inspirer of the prophets of old, but also as the present and personal guide and helper of individuals, and of the assemblies of the Church, in all their ways.

Gore's observation is worth stressing, because there is a persistent tendency, even in otherwise well-informed circles, to limit unduly the place of the Spirit in earliest Christianity. A recent scholarly book refers to Acts 2, and then to Paul's well-known caution about spiritual gifts in 1 Corinthians 14, and goes on to state, "We hear nothing further concerning spirit possession in the early Church for another century . . ."![29]

A commonly held view has it that Christianity is not a religion which emphasizes the Spirit; therefore when people claim that God's Spirit possesses them, it is an unusual occurrence. When a

---

[25] Paul's insistence here that the "rock" was Christ might be intended to qualify the claims of the Petrine circle.

[26] See Charles Gore, *The Holy Spirit and the Church* (The Reconstruction of Belief 3; New York: Scribners, 1924), 112.

[27] Gore here is referring to the baptism in Acts 19:1–7. It would be more accurate to say that they were followers of Jesus who had formerly practiced immersion only as taught by John (and Jesus himself, at first). But their baptism at Paul's hands brings with it the Holy Spirit.

[28] He here cites Acts 4:31; 6:3, 5; 11:24.

[29] Clarke Garrett, *Spirit Possession and Popular Religion: From the Camisards to the Shakers* (Baltimore: Johns Hopkins University Press, 1987), 8.

movement is styled "Pentecostalist" in the current religious scene, this designation is used to characterize the group as outside the mainstream of Christianity. But the scene of Pentecost and the scene in the house of Cornelius together demonstrate that possession by God's Spirit was understood to be fundamental to faith in Jesus and was the principal element in the experience of baptism in the name of Jesus. That is the enduring inheritance of Peter's own Pentecostalism.

The Passover of James

The influence of James, his practice, and theology were by no means limited to the circle of his followers in Jerusalem. As in the case of Pentecost and the Petrine cycle, the later history of the Church permits us to understand the development of the Christian Pascha, and that development is most plausibly associated with James.

During the second century, the Quartodeciman controversy concerning the calendar seriously divided Christians (see Eusebius, *Ecclesiastical History* 5.23–24). Most celebrated Easter on Sunday, the Lord's Day, and chose the Sunday following the time of Passover, as is the practice today. Others, chiefly in Asia Minor, followed what they cited as apostolic tradition, and broke the fast prior to Easter exactly on the fourteenth day of Nisan: the day the lambs of Passover were to be slain, then to be consumed at evening (the start of the fifteenth day of Nisan). Further, they claimed that this corresponded to the movement of the heavenly bodies, in that Passover fell precisely on the first full moon after the vernal equinox (as Passover was regularly calculated).

Here we have a tradition, according to which Passover was to be kept precisely, and is connected with astronomy. Astronomical and calendrical observance is precisely what Paul attacks in Galatians—part of the program of the group he considers to be artificially Judaizing the message of Jesus (see Galatians 4:8–11; cf. 2:14). Chief among his disputants are followers of James (Galatians 2:12).

But the principal point of contention between Paul and these Judaizers is the necessity of circumcision (Galatians 2:3–10; 5:6–12; 6:12–16). James himself seems not to have required circumcision of all believers; that is, he granted that non-Jews could be baptized, and as such were to be acknowledged as saved by Jesus (so Acts

15:13–21).[30] But by presenting the Last Supper as a Seder, James and his circle assured a continuity with Judaic practice and the calendar of Judaism that Paul resisted vociferously.

What was the motivation for this tight association of the Pascha with Passover, and how influential was it within the New Testament? By tracing the influence of James, an answer to the first question emerges clearly.

Paul's policy of including Gentiles with Jews in meals, as well as in baptism, needed the support of authorities such as Peter and Barnabas, in order to prevail against the natural conservatism of those for whom such inclusion seemed a betrayal of the purity of Israel. When representatives of James arrived in Antioch, James who was the brother of Jesus and the preeminent figure in the Jerusalem church, that natural conservatism reasserted itself. In Paul's words, Peter "separated himself," along with the rest of the Jews and even Barnabas (Galatians 2:12, 13). Jews and Gentiles again maintained distinct fellowship at meals, and Paul accuses the leadership of his own movement of hypocrisy (Galatians 2:13).

The radical quality of Paul's position needs to be appreciated. He was isolated from every other Christian Jew (by his own account in Galatians 2:11–13: James, Peter, Barnabas, and "the rest of the Jews"). His isolation required that he develop an alternative view of authority in order to justify his own practice. Within Galatians, Paul quickly articulates the distinctive approach to Scripture as authoritative that characterizes his writings as a whole. His invention of the dialectic between grace and law, between Israel as defined by faith and Israel after the flesh, became a founding principle in the intellectual evolution of Christianity through its formative period. But the eventually Pauline character of that evolution was by no means predictable at the time Paul himself wrote, and Paulinism can become an obstacle to historical study, insofar as it prevents us from imagining other forms of theological commitment to Jesus, such as that of James.

The confrontation at Antioch that Paul recounts to his audience in Galatia did not turn out happily for him at the time. His explanation of his own point of view is triumphant and ringing only in retrospect. Indeed, by the time he recollects his argument for the benefit of the Galatians (to whom he writes some four years after

---

[30] See Bruce Chilton and Craig A. Evans, eds., *James the Just and Christian Origins* (Supplements to Novum Testamentum 98; Leiden: Brill, 1999).

this confrontation), he seems so confident that one might overlook the fact that he was the loser in the battle with the representatives of James. It was he, not they, who left the area of Antioch (so Acts 15:22–41).

The position of James is not represented, as is Paul's, by a writing of James himself. But the book of Acts does clearly reflect his perspective in regard to both circumcision and the issue of purity (Acts 15), the two principal matters of concern in Galatians. The account in Acts 15 is romanticized; one sees much less of the tension and controversy which Paul attests. But once allowance has been made for the book's tendency to portray the ancient Church as a harmonious body for all its tensions, the nature and force of James's position become clear.

The two issues in dispute, circumcision and purity, are dealt with in Acts 15 as if they were the agenda of a single meeting of leaders in Jerusalem. (Paul in Galatians 2 more accurately describes the meeting he had with the leaders as distinct from a later decision to return to the question of purity.) The first item on the agenda is settled by having Peter declare that, since God gave his Holy Spirit to Gentiles who believed, no attempt should be made to add requirements such as circumcision to them (Acts 15:6–11). Believers who are named as Pharisees had insisted in contrast that "it is necessary both to circumcise them and to command them to keep the law of Moses" (15:5). The stage is now set for conflict, not only with Paul and Barnabas but with Peter. And it is Peter who, in the midst of great controversy, rehearses what happened in the house of Cornelius, which he has also just done a few chapters previously (see Acts 11:1–18; 15:7–11). Peter comes to what is not only a Pauline expression, but more particularly an expression of the Pauline school. "Through the grace of the Lord Jesus we believe to be saved, in the manner they also shall be" (Acts 15:11; see Ephesians 2:8). For that reason, it seems natural that the reference to Barnabas and Paul follows (15:12). (That order of names is no coincidence: after all, Barnabas is much better known and appreciated in Jerusalem than Paul.) Paul could scarcely have said it better himself, which is consistent with the version of Paulinism represented in Acts.

The second item on the agenda is settled on James's authority, not Peter's, and the outcome is certainly not in line with Paul's thought. James first confirms the position of Peter, but he states the position in a very different way: "Simeon has related how God first visited, to take from Gentiles a people in his name" (Acts 15:14). James's perspective here is not that all who believe are Israel (the Pauline definition), but that *in addition* to Israel God has established a people in his name. How the new people are to be regarded in relation to Israel is a question implicit in the statement, and James goes on to answer it. James develops the relationship between those taken from the Gentiles and Israel in two ways.

The first method is the use of Scripture, while the second is a requirement of purity. The logic of them both inevitably involves a rejection of Paul's position (along the lines Paul himself laid out in Galatians 2). The use of Scripture, like the argument itself, is quite unlike Paul's. James claims "with this [i.e., his statement of Peter's position] the words of the prophets agree, just as it is written" (Acts 15:15), and he goes on to cite from the book of Amos. The passage cited will concern us in a moment; the form of James's interpretation is an immediate indication of a substantial difference from Paul. As James has it, there is actual agreement between Simeon and the words of the prophets, as two people might agree: the use of the verb *sumphoneo* is nowhere else in the New Testament used in respect to Scripture. The continuity of Christian experience with Scripture is marked as a greater concern than within Paul's interpretation, and James expects that continuity to be verbal, a matter of agreement with the prophets' words, not merely with possible ways of looking at what they mean.

The citation from Amos (9:11–12, from a version virtually identical to the Septuagint, the standard Bible of Luke-Acts) comports well with James's concern that the position of the Church agree with the principal vocabulary of the prophets (Acts 15:16–17):

> After this I will come back and restore the tent [or: "hut"] of David which has fallen, and rebuild its ruins and set it up anew, that the rest of men may seek the Lord, and all the Gentiles upon whom my name is called. . . .

In the argument of James as represented here, the belief of Gentiles achieves not the redefinition of Israel (as in Paul's thought) but the restoration of the house of David. The argument is possible because a Davidic genealogy of Jesus—and, therefore, of his brother James—is assumed.

The account of James's preaching in the temple given by Hegesippus (a writer of the second century, quoted in Eusebius's *Ecclesiastical History* 2.23) represents Jesus as the Son of Man who is to come from heaven to judge the world. Those who agree cry out, "Hosanna to the Son of David!" Hegesippus shows that James's view of his brother came to be that he was related to David (as was the family generally) and was also a heavenly figure coming to judge the world. When taken together, Acts and Hegesippus indicate that James asserted Jesus was restoring the house of David because he was the agent of final judgment (the "son of man" of Daniel 7:13) and was being accepted as such by Gentiles with his Davidic pedigree.

But in James's view, Gentiles remain Gentiles; they are not to be identified with Israel. His position was not anti-Pauline (at least not in initial intention). His focus was on Jesus' role as the ultimate arbiter within the Davidic line, and there was never any question in his mind that the temple was the natural place to worship God and acknowledge Jesus. Embracing the temple as central meant for James, as it meant for everyone associated with worship there, maintaining the purity that God required in his house. Purity involved excluding Gentiles from the interior courts of the temple, where Israel sacrificed. The line of demarcation between Israel and non-Israel was no invention within the circle of James, but a natural result of seeing Jesus as the triumphant branch of the house of David.

Gentile belief in Jesus was therefore in James's understanding a confirmation of his Davidic triumph, and it did not involve a fundamental change in the status of Gentiles vis-à-vis Israel. This characterization of the Gentiles, developed by means of the reference to Amos, enabled James to proceed to his requirement of their recognition of purity. He first states, "I determine not to trouble those of the Gentiles who turn to God" (15:19), as if he were simply repeating the policy of Peter in regard to circumcision. (The implicit authority of that "I" contrasts sharply with the portrayal in Acts of apostolic decision as communal.) But he then continues that his determination is also "to write to them to abstain from the pollutions of the idols, and from fornication, and from what is strangled, and from blood" (15:20).

The rules set out by James tend naturally to separate believing Gentiles from their environment. They are to refrain from feasts in honor of the gods and from foods sacrificed to idols in the course of being butchered and sold. (The notional devotion of animals in the market to one god or another was a common practice in the Hellenistic world.) They are to observe stricter limits than usual on the type of sexual activity they might engage in, and with whom. (Gross promiscuity need not be at issue here; marriage with cousins is also included within the likely area of concern which was fashionable in the Hellenistic world and proscribed in the book of Leviticus [see chapter 18 and 20:17–21].) They are to avoid the flesh of animals that have been strangled instead of bled, and they are not to consume blood itself. The proscription of blood, of course, was basic within Judaism. And strangling an animal (as distinct from cutting its throat) increased the availability of blood in the meat. Such strictures are consistent with James's initial observation that God had taken a people from the Gentiles (15:14); they were to be similar to Israel and supportive of Israel in their distinction from the Hellenistic world at large.

The motive behind the rules is not separation as such, however. James links them to the fact that the Mosaic legislation regarding purity is widely known (15:21): "For Moses from early generations has had those preaching him city by city, as he has been read in the synagogues every Sabbath." Because the law is well known, James insists that believers, even Gentile believers, are not to live in flagrant violation of what Moses enjoined. In the words of Amos, they are to behave as "all the Gentiles upon whom my name is called." As a result of James's insistence, the meeting in Jerusalem decides to send envoys and a letter to Antioch, in order to require Gentiles to honor the prohibitions set out by James (Acts 15:22–35).

The same chapter of Leviticus that commands, "love your neighbor as yourself" (19:18), also forbids blood to be eaten (19:26) and fornication (19:29, see also 18:6–30). The canonical Epistle of James—which although pseudepigraphal nonetheless represents the thought of a circle which revered James—calls the commandment of love "the royal law" (James 2:8), acknowledging that Jesus had accorded it privilege by citing it alongside the commandment to love God as the two greatest commandments (see Mark 12:28–32). In Acts James himself, while accepting that Gentiles cannot be required to keep the whole law, insists that they should acknowledge it, by observing basic requirements concerning fornication, blood, and idolatry.[31]

---

[31] For this reason, the addition to the decree in some texts of the negative form of the Golden Rule (a form of the love commandment) is not surprising; see James Hardy Ropes, *The Text of Acts: The Acts of the Apostles III* (ed. F. J. Foakes Jackson and Kirsopp Lake; Grand Rapids: Baker, 1979), 265–69.

It is of interest that Leviticus forbids the eating of blood by sojourners as well as Israelites and associates that prohibition with how animals are to be killed for the purpose of eating (17:10–16). Moreover, a principle of exclusivity in sacrifice is trenchantly maintained: anyone, whether of Israel or a sojourner dwelling among them, who offers a sacrifice not brought to the Lord's honor in the temple is to be cut off from the people (17:8–9). In other words, the prohibitions of James, involving sacrifice, fornication, strangled meat produce, and blood, all derive easily from the very context in Leviticus from which the commandment to love is derived. They are elementary and involve an interest in what Gentiles as well as Israelites do, especially Gentiles who have a function of support within Israel.

James's prohibitions as presented in Acts are designed to show that believing Gentiles honor the law which is commonly read, without in any way changing their status as Gentiles. Thereby, the tent of David is erected again in the midst of Gentiles who show their awareness of the restoration by means of their respect for the Torah. The interpretation attributed to James involves an application of Davidic vocabulary to Jesus, as is consistent with the claim of Jesus' family to Davidic ancestry. The transfer of Davidic promises to Jesus is accomplished by accepting Scripture's terms of reference: to embrace David is to embrace Moses.

There is no trace in James's interpretation of the Pauline gambit, setting one biblical principle (justification in the manner of Abraham) against another (obedience in the manner of Moses). Where Paul divided the Scripture against itself in order to maintain the integrity of a single fellowship of Jews and Gentiles, James insisted upon the integrity of Scripture, even at the cost of separating Christians from one another. In both cases, the interpretation of Scripture was also—at the same moment as the sacred text was apprehended—a matter of social policy.

Amos 9:11 was also cited at Qumran. In one case (in 4Q174 3:10–13, a florilegium), the image of the restoration of the hut of David is associated with the promise to David in 2 Samuel 7:13–14 and with the Davidic "branch" (cf. Isaiah 11:1–10), all taken in a messianic sense. Given the expectation of a son of David as messianic king (see *Psalms of Solomon* 17:21–43), such an application of the passage in Amos, whether at Qumran or by James, is hardly strange. On the other hand, it *is* striking that the passage in Amos—particularly, "the fallen hut of David"—is applied in the *Damascus*

Document (CD 7:15–17) not to a messianic figure but to the law which is restored. Now the book of Amos itself makes Judah's contempt for the Torah a pivotal issue (Amos 2:4) and calls for a program of seeking the Lord and his ways (Amos 5:6–15), so it is perhaps not surprising that "the seeker of the law" is predicted to restore it in the *Damascus Document*. Still, CD 7:15–20 directly refers to the "books of the Torah" as "the huts of the king," interpreted by means of the "fallen hut of David." Evidently, there is a precise correspondence between the strength of the messiah and the establishment of the Torah, as is further suggested by the association with the seeker of the law *not only here,* in the *Damascus Document,* but also in the florilegium. A contextual reading of the two passages demonstrates a dual focus, on messiah and Torah in each case, such that they stand in a complementary relationship. The possibility of influence on James's interpretation of Amos as presented in Acts 15 may not be discounted.

The emphasis of James's circle on keeping the law within Jesus' movement was a powerful impetus, as we will now see, on the development of Christian insistence upon keeping Passover. It has already been explained that the actual chronology of Jesus' entry into Jerusalem at *Sukkoth* and his subsequent death prior to Passover would explain why the most basic elements of the Seder—lamb, unleavened bread, bitter herbs (see Exodus 12:8)—are notable in the narratives only for their absence. Jesus might well have expressed a desire to eat the Passover, such as Luke 22:15 attributes to him, but if so, that desire remained unfulfilled.

For all that, there is no question of any ambiguity in Matthew 26:17–19, Mark 14:12–16, and Luke 22:7–13—that pericope explicitly and emphatically presents the Last Supper as paschal. Whatever the sense of the meal originally, there is no doubt a theological investment in the Synoptics as great as Paul's (see 1 Corinthians 5:7) in presenting the meal in that light, and the Johannine timing of Jesus' death when the paschal lambs were normally slain accomplishes a similar aim (John 19:36, with Exodus 12:46). But where Paul is content to make that link in purely theological terms—by means of the metaphor that Christ is "our Pascha"—the Synoptics and John in their different ways insist upon a calendrical correspondence (although without being able to agree) between Passover and the Last Supper.

The degree of concern to link the entire complex of material related to the death of Jesus with Passover is so great throughout the sources that certainty regarding the sequence and precise timing of events is unattainable. It is clear the calendar of the early Church has vitiated the value of all the extant documents as they relate to the chronology of Jesus' death. For that very reason, they are precious beyond calculation as sources for understanding primitive Christianity's views of sacred time.

When the Synoptic pericopae specify the timing of the Last Supper, its identification as a Seder appears problematic. Matthew 26:17, Mark 14:12, and Luke 22:7 insist that Jesus' instructions to prepare to celebrate the feast in the city were given on the first day of Unleavened Bread, when the paschal lamb was slain. On any reckoning, it would be regarded as short notice, in that the lamb was to be selected on the tenth day of the month for slaughter on the fourteenth day of the month (Exodus 12:3–6). Whatever arrangements needed to be made therefore required several days prior to the feast in strictly cultic terms. The exigencies of accommodation in Jerusalem—commonly recognized to have had an infrastructure grossly inadequate for the number of its pilgrims—would no doubt have required even more notice. The paradox, then, is that the only pericopae to insist upon a paschal chronology, with the unequivocal reference to the meal as the Passover, do not make good sense in the light of that chronology.

The strain that the pericope places upon plausibility is underscored by another, more technical consideration. Commentators have observed that the reference to "the first day of the Unleavened Bread" in Mark 14:12 and Matthew 26:17 is odd, since that would presumably be Nisan 15. But the lambs were slain on Nisan 14, so that they could be eaten on the evening which marked the beginning of Nisan 15 (see *Pesachim* 1:1–4 in the Mishnah). Luke's Gospel appears both to recognize and to clean up the difficulty, by referring more fully to "the day of the Unleavened Bread, in which it was necessary to sacrifice the Pascha" (22:7). But with or without the Lukan explanation, a pericope which tries to make good sense of the considerable preparations involved in keeping Passover in Jerusalem then betrays its own credibility by confining the action to a short and ill-defined period of time. If the substance of the story seems plausible as regards to the need to arrange for clandestine meals, its chronology as a Seder appears schematic at best.

The Synoptic Gospels nonetheless proceed with the chronology developed by the pericope. The tensions involved with a narrative of Jesus' meal that originally was neither explicitly nor implicitly paschal are evident, but they would have become less striking, the greater the distance from the *actual* practices of Passover. The more Gentile the audience, the easier to accept the proposition that the meal was a Seder, because the absence of Jewish customs would be less striking.

The most severe tension is confronted in Luke, where 22:15 originally spoke of an unfulfilled desire to eat the Pascha: "And he said to them, 'With desire I desired to eat this Pascha with you before my suffering.'" It is hard to make obvious sense of this saying if one supposes Jesus is actually involved in a Seder at the time. Those who composed Luke's Gospel solved that problem by what follows in v. 16: "Because I say to you, I will no longer eat it until it is fulfilled in the kingdom of God." Luke 22:16 puts 22:15 into a new key, by having Jesus swear an oath, not to eat or drink of Passover *again* until the fulfillment of the kingdom.[32] But this Lukan gambit is only successful if Jesus is supposed in the meal *already* to be drinking fulfilled wine or eating fulfilled Pascha in the kingdom of God. This explanation fits within the theology of the Eucharist as a participation in the risen life of Christ (see Luke 24:13-35), but that theology was evidently framed after the resurrection. Luke provides a window into the considerable adjustments of meaning, which were consequent upon transforming Jesus' meal from a surrogate of sacrifice enacted near (but before) Passover into a Seder in a strict sense.

What purpose is served by the strict identification of the Last Supper as a Seder in the Synoptic Gospels? Several changes in understanding the meal are effected by a single shift of liturgical setting, however implausible its precise chronology. First, of course, the meal becomes a unique occasion within the ritual year: it is a paschal supper, and only that. Second, it is possible to keep the Passover only because Jesus makes specific preparations *in or near Jerusalem*, where it is assumed he is acquainted with at least one householder sufficiently sympathetic with his position to permit him to use a space for the celebration. Both the timing and the placement of the meal are locked into the ritual of the temple, once the paschal chronology is strictly invoked. The intentionality of Jesus' timing of the Last Supper as a Seder is underlined by the narrative.

---

[32] The gist of v. 16 is itself a traditional saying of Jesus (see v. 18, and Matthew 26:29 and Mark 14:25); what I am calling attention to here is the ordering of sayings within a new context, not the fabrication of sayings.

None of the Synoptics makes mention of the paschal lamb or its sacrifice, although they may be assumed to have been a part of the preparations envisaged, once the identification with the Seder was accepted. In any case, from the moment of Jesus' arrival there is no express reference to the Passover, except in Luke 22:15, 16, and 18 as part of a statement that Jesus will eat and drink of the paschal celebration only in the kingdom. Moreover, there is no reference to any of the constituent elements of a Seder: the roasted lamb with unleavened bread and bitter herbs (Exodus 12:8). They are all left to be inferred on the strength of the artificial context created by Matthew 26:17–19, Mark 14:12–16, and Luke 22:7–13.

The mention of singing in Matthew 26:30 and Mark 14:26 is sometimes taken as evidence of a paschal setting, and it may belong to the presentation of the meal as a Seder. In order to construe the singing in that way, however, it must be assumed that the Hallel, a sung version of some form of Psalms 113–118, is involved; even on that assumption, the Hallel was not uniquely paschal but amounted to a festal song which might be used on several occasions. Whether or not the mention of singing is part of the vignette concerning preparations for Passover, it adds nothing to the introductory setting, which is the principal instrument of the paschal presentation. That presentation makes the last meal of Jesus into a Passover, truly repeatable only once a year, and then only with the sympathetic cooperation of other Jews of sufficient wealth to provide the conditions necessary for the celebration in Jerusalem.

By a stroke of artificial context, then, the meal is more tightly linked to the liturgical year than it ever had been before, and its *only* possible occasion is in Jerusalem. Dominical meals as practiced by Peter and Paul were repeatable anywhere and frequently. The present transformation of what is now a last Passover could only truly be enacted, to use the rabbinic phrase, "between the evenings" (during the twilight of passage from one day to the next within the calendar of Judaism) of Nisan 14 and 15, and in the vicinity of the temple, where the paschal lambs were slain. If Jesus' "Last Supper" were understood as strictly paschal, its reenactment would be limited in three ways. Temporally, it would only take place at Passover; geographically, the only appropriate venue would be Jerusalem; socially, participants would need to be circumcised (see Exodus 12:48).

The last limitation appears the most dramatic, given the increasing importance of non-Jews within the Church during the course of the first century and later. By fully identifying Jesus' meal and Passover, the circle of potential participants in Eucharist excluded uncircumcised males and was limited to those who were Jews or who accepted circumcision, since circumcision was an explicit requirement for males who took part in a Seder (according to Exodus 12:48–49). Once Jesus' movement reached Gentiles, the matter of their participation in such a paschal supper would become contentious. They might have expected the Eucharistic practices of Paul and Peter to prevail, but a strict understanding of the Eucharist as a Seder would undermine any such expectation.

Problems accommodating Eucharist and Passover were in fact a feature of the early Church. A strict association of the meal and Passover lies at the heart of the Quartodeciman controversy, as we have seen. Eusebius provides the fullest account of the controversy that erupted toward the end of the second century (*Ecclesiastical History* 5.23–24). The consequence of the policy of ending the fast prior to Easter on Nisan 14 was that the day of the resurrection would often be other than Sunday, and such a practice conflicted with apostolic tradition. But such is the tenacity of Quartodeciman practice, Eusebius reports, that councils were convened in Palestine, Rome, Pontus, Gaul, Osrhoene, and Corinth (5.23).

Eusebius's claim of a cheerfully unanimous rejection of Quartodecimanism is dubious, especially in the light of his own premise that the controversy persisted in Asia. Polycrates is designated as the leader of bishops there in insisting upon the antiquity of their practice (5.24). Eusebius proceeds on documentary evidence to cite Polycrates' position in some detail. Polycrates claims that keeping the day is connected to the rising of the luminaries to meet the coming Lord and the gathering of the saints. Some of the saints are enumerated, including Philip, John, Polycarp, and Melito; it is furthermore claimed that they all kept "the day of the fourteenth of Passover according to the Gospel," as does Polycrates himself in the tradition of his kin.

Several features of Polycrates' apology invite our immediate attention, in that the strict association of Passover and Jesus' last meal—such as is achieved in Matthew 26:17–29, Mark 14:12–16, and Luke 22:7–13—would largely account for his position. The observance is indeed Quartodeciman, and in its attachment to the fourteenth day of the month, it is paschal in a calendrical sense. The calendrical observation is linked to the position of the luminaries, much as Passover was to be observed on the basis of the coincidence of a full moon and the vernal equinox. The practice is said to derive from the Gospel; a continuous tradition from the apostles allegedly derives from that evangelical mandate; the tradition is kept alive, not only in Asia, but in precisely those churches in which the Judaic environment is attested in Acts and the Pauline letters.

The Quartodecimans do not provide the cause for the association with Passover, only the assertion that it is correct (indeed, that it is both evangelical and apostolic). Eusebius would have us believe that the controversy is simply a matter of when the fast ends and the feasting begins, and that may have been the case by his time nearly two centuries later (at least in his own mind). But the heat of the controversy is such as to suggest that the identification of Jesus' Last Supper and Passover carried with it far more profound implications. Melito of Sardis, for example, dwells in his paschal homily on the correspondence between Jesus and the lamb of Passover in a manner which shows why by his time the entire language of paschal sacrifice had been appropriated by Christians.[33] The evident affinity between the Quartodecimans and Jewish practice serves to confirm that, at an earlier stage, identifying Eucharist with Passover and limiting participation within it to Jews were tendencies which went together.

The Letter to the Galatians mentions just the elements cited here as observances, practices, and beliefs to be avoided. Paul warns his readers against their observation of days, months, seasons, and years, and connects those practices to serving the "elements" of nature (4:8–11). The meaning of the term *stoikheion* as employed by Paul is not entirely certain, but it is the same word which clearly means "luminaries" in Eusebius's citation of Polycrates' position. Paul is also upset that "another gospel" should be competing with his among the Galatians (1:6–12; 2:7); he is nearly scathing in his reference to the apostolic authority of others in chapter 2 (vv. 6, 9, 11–14). He attacks those who would impose Judaic customs upon non-Jews in the name of Christ (2:14–21; 5:1–12, cf. 1:13, 14) and names Peter in particular (2:11–14); he identifies that threat with Cephas and James's followers in Antioch, who are said to have influenced Barnabas and "the rest of the Jews" (2:11–13). In aggregate, Paul opposes practices involving the observation of a calendar which themselves claim evangelical and apostolic warrant, rooted in Christian Judaism.

---

[33] For an introduction that is still useful, see F. L. Cross, *The Early Christian Fathers* (Studies in Theology; London: Duckworth, 1960), 103–9.

The fundamental dispute in which Paul was engaged, and which would take up his attention for years after the particular argument he relates, was far more profound than the simple question of dating Easter. His charge is that Cephas, Barnabas, and "the rest of the Jews" were unduly influenced by unnamed followers of James, with the result that they ceased to eat with the Gentiles and separated themselves from them (2:11–13). Quartodecimanism was a dispute regarding when to end the fast prior to the celebration of baptism and Eucharist within the Christian institution of the paschal mysteries. The archaic tradition from which it derived was based upon the custom among Christian Jews of keeping Passover and recollecting Jesus' last eucharistic meal, a custom which by the definition of Exodus 12:43–49 would exclude the uncircumcised. Circumcision is, of course, just the line of demarcation Paul in Galatians wishes to eradicate (cf. 2:3–5, 7–9, 12; 5:2, 3, 6, 11, 12; 6:13, 15).

An extension of the Torah to the Last Supper, as to a paschal meal, carried with it the consequence that "no uncircumcised man shall eat of it" (Exodus 12:48). Insofar as eucharistic meals were modeled on Jesus' final meal, exclusive fellowship would prevail then, as well, for two reasons. First, ordinary considerations of purity would make separation from non-Jews likely for Jews (as in Galatians 2:11–13). Second, even those who might permit exceptional social intercourse with non-Jews could not circumvent the strictures of the Seder. The exclusionary policy of James, as reflected in Galatians 2 and Acts 15, finds its narrative rationale in Matthew 26:17–19, Mark 14:12–16, and Luke 22:7–13: only the circumcised celebrated the last Seder, and even then only at Passover, as part of the ritual of the temple (the only place where paschal lambs could be slain).

This policy of associating Eucharist and Passover would accord with a deliberate attempt to avoid confrontation with the authorities of the temple, as well as with an insistence upon the Judaic identity of the new movement and upon Jerusalem as its center. Jerusalem became the true site of any repetition of the Lord's Supper, and then only as a domestic meal of a lamb that was slaughtered in the temple. This narrowing of eucharistic celebration to the practice of Passover would be consistent, then, with James's policy in regard to purity, Gentiles, and the Torah. Moreover, his standing within the Church, along with the supportive authority of "prophets" such as Judas and Silas (Acts 15:30–35), would explain why the Synoptics are so emphatically stamped with a paschal interpretation of Jesus' meal.

The reach of the Jacobean circle, from the group in Jerusalem to envoys such as Judas Barsabbas and Silas in Antioch, helps to explain the development of traditions associated with James. The pericope in Matthew 26:17–29, Mark 14:12–16, and Luke 22:7–13 is a frustrating mixture of plausible and implausible material. Incidental references to the preparation of a Passover in Jerusalem seem to reflect local knowledge. The disciples know that Jesus will celebrate Passover—they have only to ask where—and Jesus instructs them how to go about making the contact necessary to complete preparations. It is only the strictly chronological insistence that all those preparations were accomplished on the fourteenth day of Nisan, and that the Last Supper itself was a Seder, which strains credibility. The Jacobean tradition began by associating Jesus' final meal with the Passover for which he wanted to prepare (but did not observe). In the midst of conflict concerning the meaning of and appropriate participation in Eucharist, involving prophetic teachers such as Judas Barsabbas and Silas, the cycle of tradition apparently hardened into a chronological identification of that supper with the Seder.

The Jacobean source, as derived through Judas Barsabbas and Silas, needed to take account of paschal practice in the Diaspora. Even prior to 70 C.E., all the Jews of Antioch were scarcely in a position easily to acquire lambs which had been slaughtered in the temple. Absent such an arrangement, the only other options were (1) to revert to the domestic conception of the paschal meal (as in Exodus 12) against the provisions of Deuteronomy 16:5–7, or (2) to suppress the consumption of the lamb itself, as in later rabbinic practice. The Jacobean source, absent an explicit mention of the lamb, could proceed on the tacit understanding that, within its community, the paschal lamb was either eaten (in the vicinity of Jerusalem and elsewhere by a special cultic and commercial arrangement) or it was not (further afield). This approach would particularly come into its own following the destruction of the temple in 70 C.E. and its demolition in 135 C.E., since after these events, from the perspective of sacrifice, Jerusalem itself entered the Diaspora. The burden of the pericope is that Jesus joined with the "twelve" specifically, the signature group of the Jacobean source (cf. Mark 4:10–12), for a commemoration of Passover, and that he followed the appropriate customs. The meal was therefore marked definitively—both before and after 70 C.E.—as a Last Supper and a paschal meal.

Other festal moments

The Feast of the Dedication is explicitly mentioned in the Gospel according to John (10:22). Although there is no reason to doubt that Jesus actually did visit Jerusalem during this period,[34] John's presentation is imbued with the perspective of James. The reference appears in the midst of an extended controversy (ranging throughout chapter 10) over Jesus' self-designation as "the gate of the sheep" (10:7) and God's Son (10:31–39). The controversy over Jesus as "the gate" is also reflected in the martyrdom of James as presented by Hegesippus. Cited by Eusebius (see *Ecclesiastical History* 2.23.1–18), Hegesippus characterizes James in terms of his idiosyncratic purity in the interests of worship in the temple. He abstained from wine and animal flesh, did not cut his hair or beard, forsook oil and conventional bathing, and wore only linen garments. According to Hegesippus, those special practices gave him access even to the sanctuary. James's testimony to Jesus as the gate and as the Son results in his stoning, which is just what "the Jews" attempted to do to Jesus in the temple precincts (John 10:31).

In Hegesippus's account, James is interrogated by the authorities as he stands on a parapet of the temple: Tell us, what is the gate of Jesus? James responds with a strong declaration of Jesus as the Son of Man who will come to judge the world. The authorities then push him from the parapet and have James stoned. He is actually killed by someone with a club, who beats in his head. James's devotion to the temple and his devotion to his brother were coextensive. In each case, the focus was on the throne of God, of which Jesus was the gate and the temple the court. His court on earth was in Jerusalem, where James continued to offer worship and to insist on that purity throughout Jesus' movement, which made that worship possible and acceptable to God. The temple was the threshold to God's throne in heaven, much as in the vision of the prophet in Isaiah 6. And in the vision of James, the Son of Man associated with that throne was none other than Jesus, the gateway to heaven itself. Devotion to him and to the temple together constituted the effective worship of God.

---

[34] See Chilton, *Rabbi Jesus*, 103–23.

Loyalty to Jesus and loyalty to the temple both demanded rigorous attention to the issue of holiness, of what belongs to God in human comportment. John 10, together with Hegesippus's portrayal of James and his martyrdom, provide insight into the worship of what was in its time the most influential and public expression of faith in Jesus. Because the messiah was traditionally expected to restore true worship in the temple,[35] the Feast of the Dedication became for followers of the risen Jesus who worshiped in Jerusalem a powerful occasion of christological reflection and christological controversy.

Such is the dominance of Passover within the calendar of Christianity, *Purim* has little echo, despite its importance within Judaism. Still, Herod Antipas is pictured in Mark (6:23) as promising up to half his kingdom to little Salome, which is just what Ahasuerus repeatedly promises Esther (Esther 5:3, 6; 7:2), and trappings of power in the Herodian court are comparable with the fictional court of Ahasuerus. Of course, the events concerning John the Baptist's beheading are no *Purim,* but a terrible reversal of the heroism of an Esther or a Judith. Salome's famous dance and its result represent an antithesis of the themes of *Purim.* Although all the elements of the legend cannot be proven to be fictional, in aggregate their purpose is to exculpate Antipas from what only Antipas could be responsible for (John's death). There is an obvious analogy with the treatment of Pilate in the Gospels, where he is made to seem the dupe of the system he was in fact in charge of. In any case, it is notable that Luke's Antipas is more vigorous (see Luke 3:19–20; 9:7–9), and he makes his decision quite literally without the song and dance: Salome makes no appearance in Luke.

As the feast of *Purim* finds itself inverted in the presentation of Mark, so the destruction of the temple is treated not as an occasion of mourning but as the culmination of apocalyptic prophecy in Matthew 24–25, Mark 13, and Luke 21. In rabbinic Judaism, the destruction of the temple was remembered on the ninth of Av (the fifth month, corresponding generally to our August), an apparent compromise between the recollection of the destruction of the first temple on the seventh of Av (2 Kings 25:8–9) and of the second temple on the tenth of Av (so Josephus, *Jewish War* 6 § 250). Indeed, the compromise was already well advanced in Josephus's

---

[35] See Chilton, *The Glory of Israel: The Theology and Provenience of the Isaiah Targum* (Journal for the Study of the Old Testament: Supplement Series 23; Sheffield: JSOT, 1982), 86–96.

mind, who places both destructions on the tenth of Av. That still does not explain why the ninth triumphed as a day of fasting, and Schauss plausibly explains it as an agricultural practice, well prior to harvest.[36]

The destruction of the temple also had a signal impact on the understanding of the Day of Atonement in both Judaism and Christianity. The Mishnah's tractate *Yoma* (1:1–5:7) rehearses the meticulous preparations for this great occasion, in anticipation that the temple would function again. In the Epistle to the Hebrews (9:1–12), all the elements of sacrifice, temple, and priesthood are understood only to have foreshadowed the perfect offering of Christ, once for all. Indeed, the contrast is so strong it will serve as the point of our departure in the conclusion that follows. After the destruction of the temple the many branches of early Judaism (priestly, Essene, pharisaic, zealot, apocalyptic, prophetic) resolved themselves into what came to be known as Christianity and rabbinic Judaism. The related issues of time, calendar, and eternity proved to mark principal contrasts between these great systems, two religions divided by a common commitment to the redemption of God's people.

---

[36] Schauss, *The Jewish Festivals,* 295–96.

CHAPTER FIVE

Conclusion: breaking tyrannies of time

Two eternities: Hebrews and the mishnaic tractate *Yoma*

Texts of Judaism and Christianity represent the response of these two systems of religion to the destruction of the temple in Jerusalem. Because sacrifice there was the impetus as well as the clock of the ritual time marked out by the festivals of the year, the Roman arson in 70 C.E., and then the systematic demolition of the structure in 135 C.E., represented a violation of the very concept of sacred time, as well as the desecration of sacred space.

But instead of dispensing with the conception of temporal sanctity, Judaism and Christianity each found ways to protect time's holiness. They did so by hedging the sacred rhythm of their respective systems within an interval defined as eternity. That eternal rhythm—no longer bounded by temporal events on the ground and endlessly available to Israel or the body of Christ—was forever insulated from any further intervention of the sort the Romans had inflicted on the temple's ritual rhythm. The similarity of the Christian and Judaic responses is at first sight striking, but that kinship then attests a fundamental feature of their difference.

The *sine qua non* of the temple's function was the holy of holies. Divine residence there was especially accessed once a year—and only once a year—by the high priest alone (Leviticus 16). His appeasement for the uncleanness and sin of Israel (Leviticus 16:16) permitted atonement to be effected for the people of God in the temple throughout the year; the offerings that followed in the annual course effected the desired aims of the covenantal promises. Because that moment corresponded to the autumnal equinox, this interval indeed initiated the rhythm of sacrifice and of time in a uniquely evocative way. Classic documents of Judaism and Christianity found ways to rescue that eternal interval from the rubble left by Rome in Jerusalem.

Both the Mishnah, in the tractate *Yoma*, and the Epistle to the Hebrews (especially chapter 9) attend specifically to the high priest's visitation of the holy of holies, and each sets out—in a manner evocative of Judaism and Christianity respectively—a characteristic understanding of eternity. For the Mishnah, the interval of eternity is a matter of infinite extension; for the Epistle to the Hebrews, that interval is a single moment consuming all other moments.

Radical differences between these conceptions of eternity, articulated precisely as both documents address the meaning of the Day of Atonement, become apparent as the two texts unfold. In the case of the Epistle to the Hebrews, there is a famous argument to the effect that Jesus became a uniquely efficacious sacrifice, superseding what was offered on the Day of Atonement. Instead of an animal sacrifice, which only brings sin to mind by the repeated offering, the divine Son entered through the veil of his flesh into the true holy of holies, heaven itself, in order to offer a perpetual forgiveness by means of his blood (Hebrews 9:11–14, 24).

The identification between Jesus' death and the destruction of the temple, which the Gospels achieve in narrative terms with their reference to the tear in the temple veil (Matthew 27:51; Mark 15:38; Luke 23:45), is assumed to be complete. The passage takes it for granted that Jesus' body was a kind of "tabernacle," a locus of sacrifice where his blood was poured (Hebrews 9:11–12; see also 10:20), because the Synoptic Gospels have him speak of giving his body and blood in the Eucharist (see also John 2:21). That this argument proceeds on the assumption of the temple's destruction is as evident as the Epistle's assurance that readers will take ritual as a thing of the past, all part of the "first covenant" (Hebrews 9:18), now replaced by a "new covenant" (Hebrews 9:15). This supersession is accomplished when Jesus offers himself, making his flesh a temple, the place of sacrifice.

The crucifixion is the eternal pivot of all time. This punctiliar, timeless eternity is so much to the forefront, there is no attention whatever to the historical delay between the crucifixion and the destruction of the temple. How could that matter, when the only interval that mattered was marked by the Son's entrance to the throne of heavenly grace? Once there, this Jesus was the same yesterday, today, and forever (Hebrews 13:8). History is not yet a meaningful category in the Christian theology of Hebrews.[1]

Instead, anything meaningful derives from Christ and the throne of God (Hebrews 4:14–16; 8:1–7; 10:19–25; 12:1–2). Anything to do with the temple before Christ's enthronement was only a derivative image, a parable of the reality which can only be in heaven itself (Hebrews 10:1–18). With Hebrews, Christianity entered into the Platonic idiom of its fundamental theology, with every single institution of Judaism—be it the temple or sacrifice or prophecy or Moses or the Torah or even the angels surrounding God—depicted as types whose only function was to foreshadow the heavenly reality itself, Christ in his eternal intercession from the cross.

In stunning contrast, the Mishnaic tractate *Yoma* focuses, not on the single moment of high priestly intercession on the Day of Atonement, but on the elaborate sequence of preparatory acts leading up to and including the high priestly entry into the holy of holies. This interval begins a week before the Day, and extends through the long night of preparation and all its requirements and specific practices, with especial attention focused on the ablutions and vestments which the high priest needed in order to fulfill his unique and sacred functions.

The specifics involve the ritual regulations of the Day as well as leading up to the Day, and the framing of the high priest's dispositions, who reads or is read to all night to keep him awake (*Yoma* 1:6). Should that method fail, he is instructed to walk on a cold pavement in his bare feet, while assistants shout out to him to remain alert (*Yoma* 1:7). The carefully preserved sequence of the preparations, as well as the coordination of exterior and interior acts is striking. The reason for these features of the tractate then becomes apparent with the laconic observation that, if any of the prescribed acts is done improperly or out of order, the whole of the sequence is to be repeated, from beginning to end (*Yoma* 5:7). These acts, in other words, are to be thought through and performed in their precise sequence, or else it is as if they were not done at all.

---

[1] In regard to the invention of Christian history in relation to the Epistle to the Hebrews, see Chilton and Neusner, *Judaism in the New Testament*, 175–88, and Neusner and Chilton, *The Intellectual Foundations of Christian and Jewish Discourse*, 154–67.

Where the Epistle to the Hebrews assumes that the destruction of the temple demonstrates that its ritual has been dispensed with and replaced with Christ's offering, the tractate *Yoma* supposes that the temple's eternal routine, whatever appearances prevail, can never truly be interrupted. The holy of holies was utterly removed from Mount Zion in 135 C.E.—with the Roman demolition of the structure, the erection of a temple to Jupiter Capitolinus there, and the proscription against Jews living in Jerusalem at all. Yet however much the physical structure was lost, the heavenly structure in the imagination of the Mishnah became all the more vivid. Just as the tractate *Yoma* gives us precise details of the choreography and arrangement to prepare for and effect entry into the holy of holies, so the tractate *Middot* provides the exact dimensions of the temple as the rabbinic movement contemplated it.

The intellectual structure that could endure all also partook in a rhythmic eternity that could never be brought to a halt. One of the most obvious differences between the Mishnah and the Gospels (or any document within the New Testament) where it concerns the presentation of festivals is that the Mishnah is as systematic and precise as the Gospels are haphazard. The order of tractates called *Mo'ed* clearly provides, from the simplest Sabbath to detailed considerations of ritual in regard to participation in pilgrimage, as precise and reflective an account of sacred time as could be desired. In obvious contrast, the Gospels are famously jumbled when it concerns time, for reasons we will discuss below.

For the moment, the concern is only to emphasize that the Mishnah provides for an understanding of eternity which perdures through all time, whatever the circumstances of Israel on the ground.[2] That continuous sense of a limitless interval is articulated precisely in the tractate *Yoma,* in a way which also conveys the meditative impact that the Mishnah's contents was intended to have.

The contrast with the eternity of the Epistle to the Hebrews could not have been greater, even had it been intended. There is no literary indication that the Epistle and the Mishnah were in any

---

[2] See the comment of Jacob Neusner, "History, Time, and Paradigm in Scripture and in Judaism," *The Journal of Higher Criticism* 7.1 (2000), 54–84, 79–80:

> When we want to explain what it means to be "Israel," therefore, we appeal to not time and change but eternity and permanence. Or rather, the conception of the category, time—what is measured by the passage of the sun and moon in relationship to events here on earth—altogether loses standing.

sense speaking to one another, nor that their communities were in direct contact during the period of documentary formation. That makes their diametrical opposition over this question all the more overwhelming. The eternal interval which for Hebrews is momentary and unchanging is for the Mishnah continuous and sequential.

Weaving timeless Gospels

Once the pattern of Judaism's feasts is recognized, the failure of the Gospels to follow it systematically is manifest. This radical difference has to do with the commitment of Christianity to Christ as an eternal figure, and eternal in a way that deviates from the emerging eternity of rabbinic Judaism. The eternity that the Epistle to the Hebrews speaks of is like the tense in Greek called the aorist (or the perfect in classical Aramaic and Hebrew): an action conceived of only in itself, without reference to any grid of time. The interval of Christ's entry into a holy of holies not made by hands (Hebrews 9:11–12), unqualified by reference to any other reality, becomes the only time there is, an eternal moment: aorist eternity.

The genius of the Epistle to the Hebrews is that it discovered and articulated this principle of the Christian stance in theological terms. Once Jesus Christ is indeed seen as the same yesterday, today, and forever, one with the throne of God, the reason for his centrality within prayer and worship becomes self-evident. But Hebrews' discovery *is* a discovery, not merely a creative invention. The aorist eternity of which it speaks coherently for the first time turns out to have been influential long before Hebrews was written.

The Gospels themselves are famously confused about time (as we have noticed in this monograph more than once). It is frequently observed that the Synoptic Gospels unequivocally refer to Jesus as keeping only one feast: the final Passover in Jerusalem. Other than that, there is so little reference to anything like the course of feasts or years that it has seriously been argued that the Synoptic Gospels present Jesus' ministry as lasting less than one year.[3]

The degree of compression involved in such a conception becomes especially apparent in the Gospel according to Luke. There we find the only directly chronological reference in all the Gospels, which enables us to begin to consider the duration and time of Jesus' ministry. In the fifteenth year of Tiberius, Luke 3:1–3 seems

---

[3] See John P. Meier, *A Marginal Jew: Rethinking the Historical Jesus* (The Anchor Bible Reference Library; New York: Doubleday, 1991), 372–433.

to imply, "the word of God came to John the son of Zechariah in the wilderness," John himself was arrested (vv. 18–19), Jesus was baptized (21–22), and he began his ministry (v. 23). Scholars who have argued that Jesus' ministry lasted only a year have followed in this tradition and have crammed even more events into those eventful twelve months.

There is good reason to believe that the events need to be stretched out further over time in order to be understood. A reading of Josephus would put John's death in 21 C.E., and Jesus' execution is most plausibly placed in the time prior to Passover in the year 32 C.E.[4] The year 27 C.E. (Luke's fifteenth year of Tiberius) was indeed a fateful moment, because it marks the time when Jesus became so prominent that Herod Antipas began to seek his life, which explains why that timing was associated with the outset of Jesus' ministry.

But the compression of time represented by the Gospels, as well as their focus on the feast of Passover, marks the very purpose for which the Gospels were produced—not any attempt to write literal history. Because the texts are often more liturgical than historical, it makes little sense to treat them as chronicles or to ask whether they are successful as such.

The pivotal religious moment in the life of any Christian during the primitive and early phases of the movement was baptism. Then the believer called on God as *Abba* in the manner of Jesus, became one with Christ, joined his body, and knew the gifts of the Spirit, which proceeded from the resurrected Son of God and his Father.[5] Sources of early Christianity, after the separation of the movement from Judaism had been widely recognized, attest unequivocally that the period around Passover was still the time when, liturgically, Christians were baptized after a period of careful preparation in a catechumenate.[6] Catechumens who showed an interest in the movement could not simply be embraced as colleagues: there was

---

[4] For a development of this chronology in narrative terms, see Chilton, *Rabbi Jesus*. For a more technical discussion of the placement of John's death, see Chilton, "Recovering Jesus' *Mamzerut*," in *The New Testament and Archaeology* (ed. J. H. Charlesworth; Grand Rapids: Eerdmans, forthcoming).

[5] See Jacob Neusner and Bruce Chilton, *Jewish-Christian Debates: God, Kingdom, Messiah* (Minneapolis: Fortress, 1998), 62–66.

[6] See Thomas J. Talley, *The Origins of the Liturgical Year* (Collegeville, Minn.: The Liturgical Press, 1991), 26, 39, 163–232. Talley shows clearly that no uniformity can be claimed for a strict calendar of baptism (and much less of Lent), but he nonetheless details the paschal associations of baptism.

the danger that they might be planted by suspicious officials or distrustful religious competitors, and in any case there was no guarantee that an aspiring catechumen knew anything of Jesus that was reliable. Motives, even if not dubious, might well be misinformed.

The Synoptic Gospels are best understood as curricula for catechumens, as they would be introduced to the movement during a period of months prior to their incorporation into Christ in baptism. It is striking that the "Triple Tradition" (that is, the material all three Synoptics have in common) begins with the baptism of Jesus and concludes with the visit of Jesus' women followers to his tomb.[7]

The traditions about Jesus' birth and the details of resurrection appearances were not a part, in all probability, of basic instruction, but featured in the post-baptismal, esoteric knowledge conveyed to Jesus' followers. The season of resurrection extended to the celebration of Pentecost in the ancient Church; that would be one appropriate period to recollect appearances of the risen Jesus for the first time in a specific manner to those who had been initiated into the mystery of the Eucharist. This blend of basic instruction and more specialized knowledge seems to have been a feature of the Gospels from their origins.

Initially, Peter produced the first sustained message concerning Jesus, a message he passed on to Paul (Galatians 1:18). Within the present Synoptic Gospels, Peter's influence is palpable in the emphasis on baptism and the reception of the Spirit, a hallmark of Peter's theology. The narrative nears its climax as liturgical Passover approaches in all three texts, and Jesus' command in Gethsemane (Mark 14:38; Matthew 26:41; Luke 22:46) that Peter and his companions should remain alert is a signal of the paschal, liturgical influence of holy baptism.[8]

Together with this narrative source, the Synoptics also reflect the collection of sayings that scholars call "Q," a mishnah of Jesus' teaching on key questions, such as the kingdom of God and the appropriate conduct of apostles. The latter category of materials attests the origin of this mishnah among the group of the twelve in Jerusalem in the years immediately after Jesus' execution.

---

[7] On the development of the Gospels' cycles of tradition, see Bruce Chilton, *Profiles of a Rabbi: Synoptic Opportunities in Reading about Jesus* (Brown Judaic Studies 177; Atlanta: Scholars Press, 1989), and *A Feast of Meanings*.

[8] See John Bowman, *The Gospel of Mark: The New Christian Jewish Passover Haggadah* (Studia Post-Biblica 8; Leiden: Brill, 1965), 276–78.

Along with the Petrine message and the mishnah of the twelve, cycles of tradition such as that produced by James also need to be reckoned with, as we saw in the last chapter. James' circle tightened the connection between baptism and Passover, by presenting the inaugural Eucharist at the end of Jesus' life as an actual Seder.

Obviously, a great deal of material is not accounted for by such cycles. The tradition of James (which survived James' death), with its focal interest in the temple, probably generated what is called "the little apocalypse" (Mark 13; Matthew 24–25; Luke 21:5–36), which reflects the Roman siege against Jerusalem and the destruction of the temple.

More extensively, a wide-ranging source of Hellenistic material seems geared to the challenge of discipleship within the Greco-Roman world. Ritual purity is not required, but the purity of one's intentions is to be guarded (see Mark 7:14–23; Matthew 15:10–20). In particular, a greater faithfulness than even Peter was able to show (see Mark 14:66–72; Matthew 26:69–75; Luke 22:54–71) appears as a hallmark of the intention of this source.

In all these developments of the Synoptic tradition, there is not much trace of historical interest or chronological curiosity *per se.* All attention is focused on the unfolding of the story of God's Son as it originates publicly in his baptism and proceeds to the paschal moment, when the believer is to be baptized, as well. That moment—which in the Epistle to the Hebrews (6:1–8; 10:26–39) is the point after which there is no turning back, only further movement toward the throne of heavenly grace or rebellion—is the aorist eternity of the Synoptic Gospels, every bit as palpable (albeit less articulate) than the aorist eternity of Hebrews' Day of Atonement.

But if the Synoptic Gospels are largely atemporal in their interest in the moment which swallows up all time, the moment when the cross and baptism redeem all who would be saved, what of the Gospel according to John? Here there are three references to Passover, not just one. Does this mean Jesus' ministry lasted three years? A surprisingly large body of scholarship has argued just that.[9] I say "surprisingly," because—read in literary sequence—John's Gospel puts any notion of time out of joint.

The beautifully rational sequence of the Judaic festivals—Passover, Weeks, *Yom Kippur, Sukkoth, Chanukkah, Purim*—is dis-

---

[9] Again, see Meier, *A Marginal Jew,* 372–433.

solved in a series of references to Passover, with just a few other feasts thrown in from time to time. The Johannine roller coaster — just to mention named feasts, not inferences—runs from one Passover (2:13, 23) to another (6:4), through an unnamed feast (see 5:1, 9), then to *Sukkoth* (7:2) and *Chanukkah* (10:22), and back to Passover again (12:1; 13:1; 18:28, 39; 19:31). Two inferences from this pattern are still widely drawn, but I find both of them implausible.

According to the first, Jesus' ministry lasted three years (or four, if the unnamed feast at John 5:1 is taken as Passover, as well[10]), each of which was punctuated by a paschal pilgrimage. The feasts come in such a jumble, however, it seems spurious to suppose any exact count of them will yield a reliable chronology. All that can be safely surmised is that Jesus was associated with feasts in Jerusalem on several occasions. Because three of these were Passovers, he must have been active for *at least* three years, since we do not know if he went to Jerusalem for Passover every year.

According to the second inference, the greater number of references to festivals in John's Gospel shows that the text reflects a liturgical pattern of lectionaries for Judaic feasts. Some of the more technical reasons for doubting this claim were discussed in Chapter Two. But now we can see an even more powerful consideration against the hypothesis championed by Aileen Guilding: Passover is such a pervasive theme in John, it overwhelms any real sense of time, be it within the year or from year to year. Temporal intervals are effaced by the one Passover that matters: the Pascha of belief in Jesus.

Countless commentators on John have correctly pointed out that the signature concern of the Gospel is that those who hear or read the Gospel should continue in the faith they had already professed at baptism as they encountered the risen Jesus.[11] This is not a document for catechumens, in the style of the Synoptics, but a discourse for those who already know the basics—the Lord's Prayer and the Eucharist, for example, which John does not even recount. As a good discourse, it sets out its principal themes in its prologue

---

[10] As if, given all we have just seen, the Johannine tradents simply forgot to mention Passover! With the emphasis on water in what follows in the text, this is likely a reference to *Sukkoth,* and the material where Jesus refers to himself as the light of the world is a probable allusion to a principal theme of *Chanukkah.*

[11] See Ernst Haenchen, *John 2: A Commentary on the Gospel of John Chapters 7–21* (trans. R. W. Funk; Philadelphia: Fortress, 1980), 212–13.

(John 1:1–18) and then returns to them in the material that follows.[12] The manner in which Passover pervades the whole does not
mark time, but reveals the extent to which an ordinary sense of
time has been dissolved.

"And the word became flesh, and dwelt among us" (John 1:14)—
with that phrase, John speaks of its own aorist eternity and opens
a narrative which is ahistoric, *sub specie aeternitatis*. Like the
Mishnah, the New Testament develops a conception of eternity
in order to deal with the crushing reality of sacred time in Jerusalem having ceased with the temple's destruction. In both Judaism
and Christianity, eternity is an interval of light that permits the
rhythm of their respective systems to play through, even in the absence of the sacrificial routine which had marked time previously
for both.

In the case of Judaism, that rhythm is provided by the remembrance of the sacrificial calendar and all it involved. The Mishnah
provides exactly the kind of calendar (especially in the order of
tractates called *Mo'ed*) to which the New Testament at best alludes.
The rhythm of the continuous remembrance of an enduring recurrence of festivity makes the Mishnah's eternity a perduring interval
of light. In the case of the New Testament, as we have seen, an
aorist eternity is the rule. There was no necessity that this should
have been the case. The word become flesh, after all, was a human
life: theoretically, Christianity might have emerged with a liturgical
calendar of some thirty years on that basis. That it did not do so de-
pends not only on the circumstantial reality that the Synoptic Gospels were crafted to prepare catechumens for baptism in a year or
so. That happenstance points to the deeper, determinative factor
we can now identify.

The assurance expressed in the Epistle to the Hebrews that Jesus
Christ is the same yesterday, today, and forever echoes the Pauline
conviction that Jesus' atonement for the sins of all humanity was
made *ephapax*, "once for all" (Romans 6:10; and see the echo in
Hebrews 7:27; 9:12; 10:10). The conception of Jesus' identity and
of his salvific work is both sacrificial and instantaneous. Moreover,
both Paul and Hebrews see this aorist eternity as accessed by believers at the precise moment of baptism, the time which makes all

---

[12] See Chilton, "Typologies of Memra and the Fourth Gospel," *Targum
Studies* 1 (1992): 89–100, and *Judaic Approaches to the Gospels* (International
Studies in Formative Christianity and Judaism 2; Atlanta: Scholars Press, 1994),
177–201.

other time stand still, because one dies to sin and is raised to live before the eternal God (Romans 6:11–14; Hebrews 10:11–25). In narrative terms, the Gospels instantiate this same aorist inter-section of Jesus' nature and his salvific work. In the Synoptics, bap-tism is when Jesus is called God's Son and when the divine Spirit promised by John the Baptist breaks through from heaven (Mark 1:10–11; Matthew 3:16–17; Luke 3:22). In John's Gospel, it is the same Baptist who identifies Jesus as the Lamb and Son of God, and sees the Spirit descend upon him (John 1:29–34). A single, eternal moment links the believer, Jesus, and the Spirit of God.

The singularity of that moment feeds the New Testament's aorist conception of eternity, which plays out in a variety of ways in the documents. But there is nothing fortuitous about such a view of sa-cred time. Jesus' signature prayer itself urges that, at any time, one can pray to the *Abba* and—as one's initial act of prayer—sanctify the moment with God's name ("Hallowed be thy name," in the tra-ditional rendering; "your name will be sanctified" in a more accu-rate translation). The instant of sanctification, a *qaddish* invoking the name of God and the divine presence conveyed by the name,[13] was for Jesus not simply determined by the play of the cycles of years and jubilees, but could be focused at any moment by an eter-nity that willed to be present and exert the force of its kingdom. The aorist eternity of the New Testament, rooted in the practice of baptism, derives at the end of the day from Jesus' own spirituality.

Jesus' interval of light—the eternity that can survive the dis-ruption of ordinary time—was well suited to last beyond the de-struction of the temple. Indeed, early Christians could even, as we have seen, turn the Roman arson into a sign of the nearness of God's ultimate reign. In contrast, the philosophical challenge to the framers of the Mishnah was greater, because they were in the position of insisting upon the perdurance of the reality that to all appearances had been destroyed (while not fomenting the kind of resistance which would bring even more destruction to Israel). The dark interval addressed by the Mishnah's interval of light was the shadow cast by Rome's fist, the fact that the time as well as the space of sacrifice had been razed. In the face of this challenge, a time beyond time had to be invented, and was in fact constructed out of the elements of the sacrificial calendar.

---

[13] See Chilton, *Jesus' Prayer and Jesus' Eucharist: His Personal Practice of Spiri-tuality* (Valley Forge, Pa.: Trinity Press International, 1997), 32–36.

Christians, on the other hand, came to embrace Roman time, and not only for practical purposes.[14] They adopted the solar cycle and intensified it, because they understood Christ as the true sun.[15] In due course, the Julian calendar became the Church's, complete with the names of Roman months. When it became painfully obvious that the Julian calendar did not coincide with the cycles of the sun, Pope Gregory XIII gave his name to the calendrical reform in 1582 which shortened the year by ten days to accord with the solar cycle better. The lunar principle of the Judaic calendar was marginalized. That eloquently attests a centuries-long process, which accepts the ordinary time followed within the cultures that Christianity permeates, because an aorist eternity can be manifest in any temporal system.[16] Our "Good Friday" can take place on a day of the week named after a Norse fertility goddess, and—with some notable puritanical exceptions—no one seems much bothered.

But the adaptability of Christianity can involve confusion. As different temporal systems have been taken on through the centuries, Christians have had to be cautioned in various ways that the only time that truly matters is the eternal rhythm and interval of Christ himself. Puritanical influences are perennially (and all too lightly) dismissed as absurd, but they reflect a necessary element in the Christian conception of time: the acknowledgment that no calendar can contain the reality of God. Paul himself argued that "days and months and seasons and years" (Galatians 4:10) had nothing to do with the grace that came to believers in their baptism. As Robert Barnes of Cambridge put the matter during the sixteenth

---

[14] Indeed, Talley argues that Christians in Asia Minor observed a fixed date of Easter, April 6, on the basis of the Julian calendar, while March 25 was a competing date in Rome (see *The Origins of the Liturgical Year*, 5–13). But his hypothesis may place too much weight on the alleged difficulty of computing Passover on the basis of lunar observation.

[15] See Justin Martyr, *Apology* 67.7, and the discussion in Hugo Rahner, *Greek Myths and Christian Mystery* (trans. B. Battershaw; New York: Harper & Row, 1963).

[16] See D. J. K. O'Connell, "Calendar Reform," *New Catholic Encyclopedia* (19 vols.; New York: McGraw-Hill, 1967), 2:1065–66. As he points out, the solar orientation of the Gregorian calendar is sometimes at odds with the astronomical observance of the moon. On a grander scale, and in a philosophical idiom, Augustine worked out the temporal story of Christianity in *The City of God* (his name for the aorist eternity of the gospel) in a comprehensive history (cf. Neusner and Chilton, *The Intellectual Foundations of Christian and Jewish Discourse*, 154–67).

century, "For Christ is every day born, every day risen, every day ascended up."[17]

Rather than attempt puritanical devaluations of time—which have sometimes resulted in the prohibition of keeping Christmas and even Sundays as special times[18]—a more typical Christian reaction has been to set up, alongside the time measured out by a given culture, a different measure of time altogether: the ecclesiastical year. The emergence of such a system is itself fascinating, because it seems to provide a continuous interval through the year for what the Church holds is an eternal moment. How that occurred is a key both to Christianity's victory over time and—at the same time—to the modern incapacity to master time.

A fabric of time

When you look at the full calendar of the Christian year, with all its feast days, commemorations of saints, fasts, and special devotions, it is obvious that for the Church time is no simpler than are secular schedules. That sense of rich complication is heightened by the colors in which such calendars are printed—green, the color of most days, signaling the growth that the Spirit brings, red for martyrdom and feasts of the Holy Spirit, white for festal celebrations and saints, violet for fasting and penitence. Running a local church by such a calendar (and its variants among the liturgical denominations, whether Orthodox, Catholic, or Protestant) can seem to impose a further set of constraining intervals upon already complicated schedules.

Yet the Christian calendar has been an area of fruitful ecumenical discussion. There is a greater degree of coordination among churches than ever before in the way we observe our principal festivals and fasts, when we keep them, and the readings we use. Even more important, this coordination has been the result of more than a generation of work on the origins and practice of the calendar. Helped along by the intercontinental acceptance of the Gregorian calendar (which was only achieved during the twentieth century), an advance into ecumenical agreement has been a function in this case of scholarship and faith working together.

---

[17] Quoted from M. M. Knappen, *Tudor Puritanism: A Chapter in the History of Idealism* (Chicago: University of Chicago Press, 1939), 445, who discusses and provides the sources.

[18] See Knappen, *Tudor Puritanism*, 442–50.

That consensus has focused on the basics of the Christian year, which is our concern here. Between the first and the fourth centuries, a new way of looking at time emerged in the actual practice of the Church. This was the foundation for later developments, some of which are quite baroque.[19] Our interest here is certainly not in providing anything like a full account of the emergence of the calendar and its permutations during its long history. The influence of monastic and private practices (vital though they became) will be excluded altogether for our purpose, which needs to consider the public structuring of time by means of festival celebration.

For all its complexity, the Christian calendar is anchored in three great moments: Easter, Pentecost, and what is best termed Epiphany. Easter and Pentecost are obvious in their centrality, although we will consider the development of their Christian meaning a bit further. Reference to Epiphany, which actually commences the tripartite cycle, probably puzzles some readers, because Christmas is often thought of as the initial festival of the year. As is widely agreed, however, Christmas is a fourth-century refinement of a festival much broader in significance, a celebration of the Incarnation of God in Christ (not only of Jesus' birth) the ancient Epiphany.[20]

---

[19] See Evelyn Underhill, *Worship* (New York: Harper and Brothers, 1936); A. Allan McArthur, *The Evolution of the Christian Year* (Greenwich, Conn.: Seabury, 1953); Marion J. Hatchett, *Sanctifying Life, Time and Space: An Introduction to Liturgical Study* (A Crossroad Book; New York: Seabury, 1976); John F. Baldovin, *The Urban Character of Christian Worship: The Origins, Development, and Meaning of Stational Liturgy* (Orientalia Christiana Analecta 228; Rome: Pont. Institutum Studiorum Orientalium, 1987); Thomas J. Talley, *The Origins of the Liturgical Year* (Collegeville, Minn.: The Liturgical Press, 1991); John Harper, *The Forms and Orders of Western Liturgy from the Tenth to the Eighteenth Century: A Historical Introduction and Guide for Students and Musicians* (Oxford: Clarendon Press, 1991); Paul F. Bradshaw, *The Search for the Origins of Christian Worship: Sources and Methods for the Study of Early Liturgy* (New York: Oxford University Press, 1992); and Paul F. Bradshaw and Lawrence A. Hoffman, eds., *Passover and Easter: The Symbolic Structuring of Sacred Seasons* (Two Liturgical Traditions 6; Notre Dame, Ind.: University of Notre Dame, 1999), especially Efrat Zarren-Zohar, "From Passover to Shavuot," 71–93, and Martin F. Connell, "From Easter to Pentecost," 94–106.

[20] See Talley, *The Origins of the Liturgical Year*, 85–103. He challenges the theory of an adaptation of the *Natalis solis invicti* in Christmas. Instead he takes up an alternative explanation by Louis Duchesne: reckoning Jesus' death on March 25, and assuming the same date for his conception, December 25 becomes his birthday. *Mutatis mutandis*, the dating of April 6 corresponds to the Epiphany (see note 14 above). This hypothesis has the merit of unpacking part of the logic of the Christian calendar as it emerged, but it does not do sufficient justice to the Christian embrace of the sun and the solar cycle as images of Christ; after all, they

The term Epiphany itself means "manifestation," and refers to Christ's manifestation of God on earth; in fact, Epiphany is sometimes called "Theophany" by ancient writers.

The underlying function of this entire complex was beautifully summarized by Evelyn Underhill:

> By and in this ancient sequence, with its three great moments of Epiphany, Easter, and Pentecost, its detailed demonstration in human terms of the mysteries of Incarnation and Redemption, the Christian soul is led out through succession to a contemplation of the eternal action of God. In Christ, and therefore in all the states and acts of Christ, history and eternity meet.[21]

Such a sense of meeting eternity in a time out of time is strengthened by the practice of regular worship on Sundays. Sunday, the first day of the week, is also called the eighth day in the Christian tradition, in order to signal that, after a completed week, a week such as the one in which God created the world, a new creation commences with the resurrection of Christ.

Every Sunday is a feast of the resurrection. Its time is calculated from sundown on the Sabbath; it proceeds through the depths of the night when Christ was known to be dead and dawns with the power of new and unanticipated life. Historically, we may infer that the timing of the Christian Eucharist permitted Christian Jews to keep Sabbath and to worship Christ,[22] but such observations should not cause us to miss a more important point: Sunday signals a fresh, creative act of God in raising Jesus. Christians meet then to join themselves to that divine creativity, in a time which takes them out of ordinary time and into an experience of eternity.

For just this reason, Easter is always celebrated on a Sunday. The ancient connection to the paschal season is retained (and paschal language is employed to speak of Jesus' death and resurrection), but what is celebrated is the resurrection, not Israel's liberation

---

had been worshiping on the day called by the name of the sun at dawn, applying the imagery of Malachi 4:2 to Jesus (cf. Luke 1:78–79!), and facing east for prayer (see Tertullian, *Ad Nationes* 1.13) long before the emergence of Christmas. Talley is extremely helpful in warning against the assumption of a purely mechanical (and political) embrace of a Roman holiday by early Christians, but their devotion to Christ as their sun before the time of Constantine must have been an influential factor in the development of their calendar.

[21] Underhill, *Worship*, 73.

[22] See, for example, Larry W. Hurtado, *At the Origins of Christian Worship: The Context and Character of Earliest Christian Devotion* (Grand Rapids: Eerdmans, 2000).

from Egypt as such. Passover was computed prior to the fourth century C.E. by beginning with the first new moon after the spring equinox, and counting fourteen days (to the full moon). Easter is computed by taking the Sunday following the full moon after the equinox. Because the Orthodox Church has never accepted the Gregorian reform of the calendar, its Easter and the West's do not match up.[23] So the two Easters and Passover are always within reach of another, and yet doggedly out of phase.

The paschal season became the normative period for the final instruction and preparation of catechumens for baptism. As a result, a time of fasting prior to Easter was observed, although the season now called Lent only emerged slowly and was kept for various lengths of time. Fasting (especially on Wednesdays and Fridays, in deliberate distinction from Jewish fasts on Tuesdays and Thursdays) was a characteristic feature of early Christian devotion from the second century.[24] Its aim was to focus prayer and also to prepare the believer for the spiritual celebration to come on Sunday. During Lent, an emphasis on repentance (following the theme of John's baptism) was also very strong.

Because Easter is always on a Sunday, Christian Pentecost—seven weeks (or fifty days) later—also falls on a Sunday. Its great theme of the endowment of Spirit which comes from the risen Christ obvi-

---

[23] Both Orthodoxy and the West follow a canon from the the Council of Nicea, which fixes Easter on the Sunday following the full moon after the equinox (and so, between March 22 and April 25). At that time, Jewish practice continued to set the month of Nisan from the new moon following the equinox (see *Rosh Hashanah* 1:3–5; 2:2–4 in the Mishnah), so that Easter and Passover (Nisan15) often fell in different weeks. The regularization of the calendar of Judaism is often attributed to Hillel II in 358–359 C.E., but the detailed reckoning of dates probably only emerged during the tenth century. (See Ephraim Jehudah Wiesenberg, "Calendar," 5:43–50.) In 525 C.E., Dionysius Exiguus set out tables for the dates of Easter within the Julian calendar, which had been promulgated in 45 B.C.E. In so doing, he established a Christian scheme of chronology ("B.C." and "A.D.") that is still in use. Although Pope Gregory XIII published a revision of the Julian calendar in 1582, England and America did not accept this calendar until 1752, and Orthodoxy still resists it (perhaps mindful that Lenin imposed the Gregorian calendar on the fledgling Soviet Union). A dated and fixed Sunday has been proposed to deal with the problem, but a cleaner, more fully ecumenical solution would be to date Easter as the Sunday following Passover, in accordance with ancient practice (and quite aside from the Julian and Gregorian calendars).

[24] See the still useful discussion in C. Taylor, *The Teaching of the Twelve Apostles* (Cambridge: Deighton Bell, 1886), 58–62, citing chapter 8 of the *Didache,* a document that also establishes the Christian practice of Sunday (see *Didache* 14).

ously links it inextricably with Easter, making any sense of the wheat harvest or even the giving of the covenant and the law (as in *Shavuoth*) residual. Just as the Christian Paschal Mysteries are a signal development—not only a repetition of Passover—so Pentecost can be related typologically to the Judaic feast, although a radically different character also needs to be acknowledged. Yet the fact is that celebrations of the Holy Spirit in Christianity have often occurred during the summer months in the northern hemisphere, and there are many examples of informal, local festivals during that time of the year.

Much as Christianity could relate typologically to Judaism in its Easter and its Pentecost, understanding Christ as the hidden reality between the ancient types of Exodus and covenant, so Christians could absorb the symbols, images, and festivals of other cultures as types. That absorption has fed the variety of Christian theology, and contributed signally to what is today a very complex calendar which has grown out of the Julian calendar of the Roman Empire and its eventual revision. For the most part, those developments (such as the much-commented-upon day of St. Valentine) do not concern us here. But when it comes to Epiphany, we face the stark fact of that absorption at an extremely early period.

There is good evidence to support the analysis that Epiphany has been kept from the time of the second century, and a case has been made that its emergence is even signaled in the Gospel according to John (ca. 100 C.E.). January 6 had been an ancient Egyptian feast of the goddess *Aion*, kept at what was once thought to be the time of the winter solstice.[25] This celebration was also associated with the god Dionysus, and his mythic capacity to turn water into wine. Christians at that time kept that day as the dawn of their light into the world, especially when Jesus was baptized. A. Allan McArthur argues that John's Gospel—in its references in the opening section (John 1:1–2:11) to light, baptism, and Jesus' visit to Cana—marks the emergence of the Christian Epiphany.[26]

The great strength of McArthur's reading, in addition to its advantage in explaining the emergence of a central Christian feast, is that it accounts for the atemporal orientation of John's

---

[25] For an illuminating discussion of the evidence, see Talley, *The Origins of the Liturgical Year*, 103–47. Without entering here into a detailed discussion of his argument, I would observe that at the origins of Epiphany in the solar associations with Jesus seem stronger than any historical assertion about his birth.

[26] McArthur, *The Evolution of the Christian Year*, 58–69.

Gospel.[27] As a compressed discourse during a festal period, conscious that much more might be said (John 20:30), designed to vivify the sense of the Epiphany in the minds of believers who had already been baptized the previous Easter or earlier, the purpose and occasion of John's poetic power would become plain. In that the goddess *Aion* was also known as "Time" *(Kronia)*, Epiphany also marks the beginning of the year, and of time itself.

Whether or not Epiphany was the occasion of John's gospel around 100 C.E., Epiphany was certainly a principal feast of the Church during the second century. Its emergence marked the structural completion of the Christian year. In several ways, it conveyed the aorist eternity of the Gospels by syncopating the intervals of time that it flowed through. On a weekly basis, the eighth day, the moment of newly creative resurrection, was celebrated in the Eucharist. Annually, the newly-defined feasts of Easter and Pentecost took up the combined solar and lunar definition of the Judaic feasts of *Pesach* and *Shavuoth,* but it conformed them both to the observation of Sunday. In the case of Epiphany, however, the calculation on an entirely solar, pagan basis was accepted, so that the entire annual complex of Epiphany, Easter, and Pentecost regularly followed no single scheme of computation. Further, the Christian cycle began much earlier, with the winter Epiphany, than the Roman new year, which began in the spring.[28]

The pattern of the year was even syncopated within its internal observation. Epiphany and Easter were prefaced with a period of preparation and fasting (Advent and Lent respectively), but Pentecost pressed in on the heels of Easter, without penitential preface. Ancient formularies especially mark this change, by solemnly *forbidding* that anyone should kneel between Easter and Pentecost. One was to stand and praise God in embracing the glad news of resurrection.

The eclipse of the interval of light

The uncompromising simplicity of this scheme was recognized in a seminal and deeply influential work by Dom Gregory Dix,[29]

---

[27] Talley (*The Origins of the Liturgical Year,* 121) also commends McArthur's theory of an Epiphany reading of John, although he is skeptical of the pagan origins of the festival.

[28] See Talley, *The Origins of the Liturgical Year,* 80–81.

[29] Dix, *The Shape of the Liturgy* (London: Dacre Press, 1945).

seconded by the daring and incisive amendment of McArthur.[30] Taken together, these two works set the agenda of the reform of the liturgical calendar in Western Christendom during the twentieth century. That work was especially carried out in the United States under the influence of Marion Hatchett,[31] in the context of revising the Episcopal Book of Common Prayer, a program which was taken up in the Roman Catholic Church after the Second Vatican Council as well as in the Church of England. As I have already remarked, the success of this renewal of liturgical practice is unprecedented for the degree of consensus it has involved, as well as for the combination of genuine scholarship and ecclesiastical diplomacy it has occasioned.

But it would be a pity for Christianity, having won so signal an ecumenical victory, to lose the war over time. There has been a tendency in the calendar of the Church to miss the syncopations which have been so carefully devised by theology and practice. McArthur sees this process as beginning in the break-up of the liturgical year into discrete occasions, and his observation is a useful caution against burdening worship with too much historical reminiscence, since the focus of worship is eternity.[32]

This tendency toward too much historicism is not merely a happenstance in the development of the Church, but represents a perennial problem, which at the end of the day concerns time. The problem emerged clearly during the fourth century, just as the present Christian calendar took on its definite structure.

These adjustments were properly theological in their intent. Epiphany was to celebrate not just baptism but the fact of God Incarnate from the moment of Jesus' birth (Christmas). The Jesus encountered in the Easter miracle needed to be acknowledged as having truly died (Good Friday). The Spirit poured out by Jesus at Pentecost came from the divine Throne to which he had mounted

---

[30] *The Evolution of the Christian Year.*

[31] For example, see his *Commentary on the American Prayer Book* (New York: Seabury Press, 1980).

[32] McArthur sounds this note thematically in *The Evolution of the Christian Year* (see p. 10):

> Thus the primitive liturgical year consisted of three unitive festivals, Epiphany, Pascha, and Pentecost. In the fourth century three new festivals were established—Christmas, Good Friday and Ascension Day. The resultant process of evolution broke down the unitive nature of the older commemorations. It is the six festivals of Christmas, Epiphany, Good Friday, Easter, Ascension, and Pentecost that constitute the permanent structure of the Christian Year.

(the Ascension). In effect, the calendar permitted the great creeds of Christendom to be interpreted actively in the worship of the community.

But the fourth century also saw a very strong tendency to suppose that the eternity of the Gospels had entered forever *into* human time. The emperor's conversion was described as an apocalypse, and Constantine was compared with Christ himself. These were not just expressions of popular enthusiasm, but the assertions of Eusebius—bishop, theologian, and the father of ecclesiastical history.[33]

Dix observed the results within the development of the eucharistic liturgy:

> As the church came to feel at home in the world, so she became reconciled to *time*. The eschatological emphasis in the eucharist inevitably faded. It ceased to be regarded primarily as a rite which manifested and secured the *eternal consequences* of redemption, a rite which by manifesting their true being as eternally "redeemed" momentarily transported those who took part in it beyond an alien and hostile world of time into the Kingdom of God and the World to come. Instead, the eucharist came to be thought of primarily as the representation, the enactment before God, of the *historical process* of redemption.[34]

Time on such an understanding seems to be totally baptized by eternity, as if one were living in the moment of ultimate judgment and vindication. Many Christians conceived of matters in that way. For that reason, the inevitable setbacks of the Empire, most notably Alaric's sack of Rome in 410 C.E., were more than embarrassments. They shook to its foundations the faith that the Empire and human time itself had entered into eternity.

In response to that crisis, Augustine of Hippo, the most influential theologian in the West, wrote *The City of God*. Because God's city was the dominion of love, timeless and enduring, human cities could only approximate it, soldiering on until such a moment as heaven's eternity truly did become all in all. With Augustine, a normative Christian history was born, as well as a skepticism that ordinary, human time could be definitive.

A consequence of Augustinian time is that the end—the end of one's life, the end of history—is the occasion of ultimate judgment. That did not in any sense reduce Augustine's own awareness that

---

[33] See Neusner and Chilton, *The Intellectual Foundations of Christian and Jewish Discourse*, 154–61.

[34] Dix, *The Shape of the Liturgy*, 305.

eternity could be experienced at any moment, and his treatise on the Trinity precisely focuses on how God can be known, however proximately, by means of disciplined contemplation.

Without such contemplation, however, the interval of human time until judgment comes can be portrayed as a necessarily dark interval. The darkness was as thick as hell for those in the Middle Ages who believed that their own existence was purgatorial until the moment of death (at least), and made monasticism the one reliable relief from the tyranny of being mortal. It is that tyranny, the tyranny of time which is dominated by finite intervals but without eternity, without rhythm, which is the secular inheritance of medieval hell. Time as endless constraint, the problem of time as described in our first two chapters, is nothing other than Augustinian history without Augustinian contemplation.

Restoring time

Space for that contemplation was and is created within Christianity by the focus of faith on the aorist eternity of Christ's sacrifice. That brings him into the very presence of God, and all those who believe in him may follow. As we have seen, eternity may be differently conceived, and Judaism in particular constructed a continuous alternative to Christianity's timeless moment. Similar contrasts with Buddhism, Hinduism, and Islam might be developed, but that obviously would take us well beyond our compass here.

Our consideration suggests that the eternities conveyed by the liturgical calendars of Christianity and Judaism now have a framework within which they may be better understood. Here, we have let the texts tell their own story of time, but within the context of the theoretical discussion of the problem of time in the opening two chapters. Side by side with such a philosophical approach, scientific considerations have totally reopened the issue of time.

In a recent book, John Templeton summarized seminal developments beyond Einstein's Relativity. As he reports the present state of affairs, the possibility has emerged that time itself is no constant dimension, but blurs with the dimensions of space.[35] That is, time appears to be an artifact of the world's genesis, rather than its framework. It is in that sense constructed out of eternity, in a way that to Templeton's mind is consistent with theism. Precisely, at this

---

[35] Templeton, *Possibilities for Over One Hundredfold More Spiritual Information* (Philadelphia and London: Templeton Foundation, 2000), 95.

point, eternity has a future, in that it no longer appears to be pressed out by science but to be part of the ground of scientific scrutiny.

Theories involving many dimensions beyond those we presently recognize abound in theoretical literature, and some commentators believe they will revolutionize our vision of the world, our science, and our organic lives during the new century.[36] Whether or not that proves to be the case, what is plain is that, in the intellectual world after Relativity, there is a consensus that time is not a changeless constraint, but a figment of larger realities. With that the calendrical eternities of Judaism and Christianity can only agree, and they actually put into practice what for others is a matter of speculation.

---

[36] See Michio Kaku, *Visions: How Science Will Revolutionize the 21st Century* (New York: Anchor, 1998).

Epilogue

This book began with an analysis of how time's constraint has cramped our understanding of humanity in the part of the world that likes to think of itself as developed. Constraint was seen to stem from the dominance of time as interval over time as rhythm. This observation took us into the coordinated awareness of time—enacting a *mimesis* of both rhythm and interval—within sacrificial worship and the arts. The calendar of ancient Israel showed us how such a rhythmic interval of sustained and sustaining sacrifice shaped a culture and produced a distinctive view of time. Primitive Christianity was imbued with that calendar, and especially embraced the eschatological emphasis on a final sacrifice that would fulfill all time even as it would sanctify all space. The legacies of Jesus, Peter, and James reflect distinctive theories and practices of that hope for the transformation of human existence that their gospel represented.

As both Judaism and Christianity confronted the destruction of the temple in 70 C.E., they discovered resources that enabled them to survive the shattering of their sacred clock. The interval once marked by sacrifice in Jerusalem was replaced by an eternal interval, either the perduring round of feasts recollected from the Torah, or Jesus' offering of himself once for all upon the cross. Each religion shaped an interval of light, a distinctive eternity, out of dark disaster.

Our roots are in these ancient cultures, and many of us put their wisdoms into contemporary practice. As I worked on this book, the kafuffle over an impending meltdown of the world's computers on January 1, 2000, sometimes struck me as comic. Journalists whipped up a crisis before the crisis itself came, and then it did not happen anything like as predicted. This disappointed apocalypse in secular time exemplified our love and hate and fear of time's constraint, as well as our capacity to turn our ambivalence into pseudotechnical language. "Y2K" was a dud.

Since then, simple numbers have come to haunt us. "9-11" is a date as well as the emergency number of most American telephones. The assault that day could only have been produced by the ruthless observation of intervals—the times of flights, the number of available seats, the amount of fuel carried, where security might be weak, the distances to be covered, what sequence of actions would bring airliners to their targets, the body count of likely victims at the moment of impact.

"Know that the gardens of paradise are waiting for you in all their beauty": these words, found in the letter designed to motivate the hijackers in their precise sequence of actions, makes it clear that eternity was promised in exchange for their crime. Islam, no less than Judaism and Christianity (and come to that, Hinduism and Buddhism), has found not only the resources to address disaster on the ground, but also militants who answer disaster with forms of mayhem that they believe are divinely sanctioned.

Whatever the motivation for the crimes, those in the World Trade Center and the Pentagon and the hijacked planes were victims of constraints deliberately calculated in time. Their families and friends are marked indelibly by the crimes and the losses. Many of us who remember the Twin Towers see them fall again and again in our troubled sleep, a repetitive transcendence of time we would like to do without.

The response to terror brings its own constraints; in this case some of us need to observe the seasons (natural and religious) when war can be conducted in Afghanistan, others calculate the incubation period of anthrax; the number of innocent casualties our actions might inflict concerns us all. The constraints of time, heightened by fear and anger, produce victims in response to victims.

Yet countless acts of genuine and sometimes heroic humanity which "9-11" brought forth—from firefighters and passengers and police and politicians and neighbors and workers and medics—show that no person on that day was merely a victim. Whatever the constraints of a temporal hell in which there appeared to be no room at all for humanity, they discovered a rhythm of action to react—however briefly—as human beings.

Pressed to the limit by calculations designed to reduce them to nothing, they discovered the interval of light that makes eternity possible. To some extent, the physiological sharpness that seems to slow time down during our reaction to danger helped them. But we must also weigh the influence of millennia of religious practice and belief. The enduring Torah, the timeless Christ—along with their myriad reflections in philosophy and art and belief, and their counterparts in the other global religions—have on many occasions shattered the illusions of this world and this world's pretense to dominion over time. The dark interval whose consequences remain to be worked out fully, however dreadful, is not equal in power to that interval of light that shines through the wisdom of our faith.

Selected Bibliography

Ahlstrom, Sydney E. *A Religious History of the American People.* New Haven: Yale University Press, 1973.

Ahlstrom, Sydney E., ed. *Theology in America: The Major Protestant Voices From Puritanism to Neo-Orthodoxy.* The American Heritage Series. Indianapolis: Bobbs-Merrill, 1967.

Baldovin, John F. *The Urban Character of Christian Worship: The Origins, Development, and Meaning of Stational Liturgy.* Orientalia Christiana Analecta 228. Rome: Pont. Institutum Studiorum Orientalium, 1987.

Barr, James. *Fundamentalism.* Philadelphia: Westminster, 1977.

———. *The Semantics of Biblical Language.* London: Oxford University Press, 1961.

Barrett, C. K. *The Acts of the Apostles I.* The International Critical Commentary. Edinburgh: Clark, 1994.

Bloch, Abraham P. *The Biblical and Historical Background of Jewish Customs and Ceremonies.* New York: Ktav, 1980.

———. *The Biblical and Historical Background of the Jewish Holy Days.* New York: Ktav, 1978.

Boman, Thorleif. *Hebrew Thought Compared with Greek.* Translated by J. L. Moreau. The Library of History and Doctrine. Philadelphia: Westminster, 1960.

Bowman, John. *The Gospel of Mark: The New Christian Jewish Passover Haggadah.* Studia Post-Biblica 8. Leiden: Brill, 1965.

de Boyer de Sainte Suzanne, Raymond. *Alfred Loisy, entre la foi de l'incroyance.* Paris: Centurion, 1968.

Bradshaw, Paul F. *The Search for the Origins of Christian Worship: Sources and Methods for the Study of Early Liturgy.* New York: Oxford University Press, 1992.

Bradshaw, Paul F., and Lawrence A. Hoffman, eds. *Passover and Easter: The Symbolic Structuring of Sacred Seasons*. Two Liturgical Traditions 6. Notre Dame, Ind.: University of Notre Dame, 1999.

Brown, George W., and Tirril Harris. *Social Origins of Depression: A Study of Psychiatric Disorder in Women*. New York: Free Press, 1978.

Budd, Malcom. *Music and the Emotions: The Philosophical Theories*. London: Routledge, 1992.

Cathcart, Kevin J., and Robert P. Gordon. *The Targum of the Minor Prophets*. The Aramaic Bible 14. Wilmington: Glazier, 1989.

Chilton, Bruce. *A Feast of Meanings: Eucharistic Theologies from Jesus through Johannine Circles*. Supplements to Novum Testamentum 72. Leiden: Brill, 1994.

———. *The Glory of Israel: The Theology and Provenience of the Isaiah Targum*. Journal for the Study of the Old Testament: Supplement Series 23. Sheffield: JSOT, 1982.

———. *Jesus' Prayer and Jesus' Eucharist: His Personal Practice of Spirituality*. Valley Forge, Pa.: Trinity Press International, 1997.

———. *Judaic Approaches to the Gospels*. International Studies in Formative Christianity and Judaism 2. Atlanta: Scholars Press, 1994.

———. "Judaism." Pages 398–405 in *Dictionary of Jesus and the Gospels*. Edited by J. B. Green, S. McKnight, and I. H. Howard. Downers Grove, Ind.: InterVarsity, 1992.

———. *Profiles of a Rabbi: Synoptic Opportunities in Reading about Jesus*. Brown Judaic Studies 177. Atlanta: Scholars Press, 1989.

———. *Pure Kingdom: Jesus' Vision of God*. Studying the Historical Jesus 1. Grand Rapids: Eerdmans, 1996.

———. *Rabbi Jesus: An Intimate Biography*. New York: Doubleday, 2000.

———. "Recovering Jesus' *Mamzerut*." *The New Testament and Archaeology*. Edited by J. H. Charlesworth. Grand Rapids: Eerdmans, forthcoming.

———. *The Temple of Jesus: His Sacrificial Program within a Cultural History of Sacrifice*. University Park, Pa.: The Pennsylvania State University Press, 1992.

———. "The Transfiguration: Dominical Assurance and Apostolic Vision." *New Testament Studies* 27 (1980): 115–124.

Chilton, Bruce, and Craig A. Evans, eds. *James the Just and Christian Origins*. Supplements to Novum Testamentum 98. Leiden: Brill, 1999.

Collins, John J. "Sibylline Oracles: A New Translation and Introduction." Pages 317–472 in vol. 1 of *The Old Testament*

Pseudepigrapha. Edited by J. H. Charlesworth. 2 vols. Garden City, N.Y.: Doubleday, 1983.

Cross, F. L. *The Early Christian Fathers*. Studies in Theology. London: Duckworth, 1960.

Docker, John. *Postmodernism and Popular Culture: A Cultural History*. Cambridge: Cambridge University Press, 1994.

Friberg, Jöram. "Numbers and Counting." Pages 1139–46 in vol. 4 of *Anchor Bible Dictionary*. Edited by D. N. Freedman. 6 vols. New York; Doubleday, 1992.

Girard, René. *The Scapegoat*. Translated by Yvonne Freccero. Baltimore: Johns Hopkins University Press, 1986.

Gore, Charles. *The Holy Spirit and the Church*. The Reconstruction of Belief 3. New York: Scribners, 1924.

Gottsch, John D. "Mutation, Selection, And Vertical Transmission of Theistic Memes in Religious Canons." *Journal of Memetics - Evolutionary Models of Information Transmission* 5 (2001) (www.cpm .mmu.ac.uk/jom-emit/2001/vol5/gottsch_jd.html).

Haenchen, Ernst. *John 2: A Commentary on the Gospel of John Chapters 7–21*. Translated by R. W. Funk. Phildadelphia: Fortress, 1980.

Harper, John. *The Forms and Orders of Western Liturgy from the Tenth to the Eighteenth Century: A Historical Introduction and Guide for Students and Musicians*. Oxford: Clarendon Press, 1991.

Hartman, Lars. *"Into the Name of the Lord Jesus": Baptism in the Early Church*. Studies of the New Testament and Its World. Edinburgh: T&T Clark, 1997.

Hatchett, Marion J. *Sanctifying Life, Time and Space: An Introduction to Liturgical Study*. A Crossroad Book. New York: Seabury, 1976.

Himmelfarb, Gertrude. *The New History and the Old*. Cambridge, Mass.: Belknap, 1987.

Hurtado, Larry W. *At the Origins of Christian Worship: The Context and Character of Earliest Christian Devotion*. Grand Rapids: Eerdmans, 2000.

Kaku, Michio. *Visions: How Science Will Revolutionize the 21st Century*. New York: Anchor, 1998.

Karp, David A. *Speaking of Sadness: Depression, Disconnection, and the Meanings of Illness*. New York: Oxford University Press, 1996.

Kivy, Peter. *The Fine Art of Repetition: Essays in the Philosophy of Music*. Cambridge: Cambridge University Press, 1993.

Knappen, M. M. *Tudor Puritanism: A Chapter in the History of Idealism*. Chicago: University of Chicago Press, 1939.

Lake, Kirsopp. "The Apostolic Council of Jerusalem." Pages 195–212 in vol. 5 of *The Beginnings of Christianity*. Edited by F. J. Foakes Jackson and Kirsopp Lake. 5 vols. Grand Rapids: Baker, 1979.

Lane, William L. *The Gospel according to Mark*. London: Marshall, Morgan & Scott, 1974.

Levine, B. A. "Priestly Writers." Pages 683–87 in *The Interpreter's Dictionary of the Bible, Supplementary Volume*. Edited by K. Crim. Nashville: Abingdon, 1976.

Lucas, D. W. *Aristotle, Poetics*. Oxford: Clarendon, 1972.

Mann, J. "The Observance of the Sabbath and the Festivals in the First Two Centuries of the Current Era according to Philo, Josephus, the New Testament and the Rabbinic Sources." *The Jewish Review* 4 (1914): 433–56, 498–532.

Manson, T. W. "The Cleansing of the Temple." *Bulletin of the John Rylands Library* 33 (1951): 271–82.

McArthur, A. Allan. *The Evolution of the Christian Year*. Greenwich, Conn.: Seabury, 1953.

Meier, John P. *A Marginal Jew: Rethinking the Historical Jesus*. The Anchor Bible Reference Library. New York: Doubleday, 1991.

Milgrom, Jacob. "Priestly ("P") Source." Pages 454–61 in vol. 5 of *Anchor Bible Dictionary*. Edited by D. N. Freedman. 6 vols. New York: Doubleday, 1992.

Morris, L. *The New Testament and the Jewish Lectionaries*. London: Tyndale, 1964.

Nancy, Jean-Luc. "Sharing Voices." Pages 211–59 in *Transforming the Hermeneutic Context: From Nietzsche to Nancy*. Intersections: Philosophy and Critical Theory. Albany: State University of New York, 1990.

Neusner, Jacob. "History, Time, and Paradigm in Scripture and in Judaism." *The Journal of Higher Criticism* 7.1 (2000): 54–84.

———. *The Mishnah: A New Translation*. New Haven: Yale University Press, 1988.

———. *The Presence of the Past, the Pastness of the Present: History, Time, and Paradigm in Rabbinic Judaism*. Bethesda, Md.: CDL Press, 1966.

———. *The Talmud of Babylonia: An Academic Commentary. Vol. 29, Menahoth*. South Florida Academic Commentary Series 23. Atlanta: Scholars Press, 1996.

Neusner, Jacob, and Bruce Chilton. *Christianity and Judaism: The Formative Categories*. 3 vols. Harrisburg, Pa.: Trinity Press International, 1995–1997.

———. *The Intellectual Foundations of Christian and Jewish Discourse: The Philosophy of Religious Argument.* London: Routledge, 1997.

———. *Jewish-Christian Debates: God, Kingdom, Messiah.* Minneapolis: Fortress, 1998.

———. *Judaism in the New Testament: Practices and Beliefs.* London and New York: Routledge, 1995.

———. *The Presence of the Past, the Pastness of the Present: History, Time, and Paradigm in Rabbinic Judaism.* Bethesda: CDL Press, 1996.

———. *Trading Places: The Intersecting Histories of Judaism and Christianity.* Cleveland: Pilgrim, 1996.

———. *Types of Authority in Formative Judaism and Christianity.* London: Routledge, 1999.

Neusner, Jacob, Bruce Chilton, Andrew M. Greeley, and William Scott Green. *Forging a Common Future: Catholic, Judaic, and Protestant Relations for a New Millennium.* Cleveland: Pilgrim, 1997.

O'Connell, D. J. K. "Calendar Reform." Pages 1065–66 in vol. 2 of *New Catholic Encyclopedia.* 19 vols. New York: McGraw-Hill, 1967.

Pummer, Reinhard. *The Samaritans.* Iconography of Religions 25.5. Leiden: Brill, 1987.

Rahn, Jay. *A Theory for All Music: Problems and Solutions in the Analysis of Non-Western Forms.* Toronto: University of Toronto Press, 1983.

Rahner, Hugo. *Greek Myths and Christian Mystery.* Translated by B. Battershaw. New York: Harper & Row, 1963.

ReQua, Eloise G., and Jane Statham. *The Developing Nations: A Guide to Information Sources.* Management Information Guide 5. Detroit: Gale, 1965.

Rochber-Halton, F. "Calendars." Pages 810–14 in vol. 1 of *Anchor Bible Dictionary.* Edited by D. N. Freedman. 6 vols. New York: Doubleday, 1992.

Ropes, James Hardy. *The Text of Acts: The Acts of the Apostles III.* Edited by F. J. Foakes Jackson and Kirsopp Lake. 5 vols. Grand Rapids: Baker, 1979.

Schauss, H. *The Jewish Festivals: History and Observance.* Translated by S. Jaffe. New York: Schocken, 1962.

Sharpe, D. R. *Walter Rauschenbusch.* New York: Macmillan, 1942.

Silverstein, Brett, and Deborah Perlick. *The Cost of Competence: Why Inequality Causes Depression, Eating Disorders, and Illness in Women.* New York: Oxford University Press, 1995.

Smart, J. J. C. "Time." Pages 126–34 in vol. 8 of *The Encyclopedia of Philosophy*. Edited by P. Edwards. 8 vols. New York: Macmillan and The Free Press, 1967.

Squires, John T. *The Plan of God in Luke-Acts*. Society for New Testament Studies Monograph Series 76. Cambridge: Cambridge University Press, 1993.

Stanier, R. Y., et al. *The Microbial World*. Englewood Cliffs, N.J.: Prentice-Hall, 1986.

Talley, Thomas J. *The Origins of the Liturgical Year*. Collegeville, Minn.: The Liturgical Press, 1991.

Tarasti, Eero. *A Theory of Musical Semiotics*. Advances in Semiotics. Bloomington and Indianaoplis: Indiana University Press, 1994.

Taylor, C. *The Teaching of the Twelve Apostles*. Cambridge: Deighton Bell, 1886.

Templeton, John. *Possibilities for Over One Hundredfold More Spiritual Information*. Philadelphia and London: Templeton Foundation, 2000.

Torgovnich, Marianna. *Gone Primitive: Savage Intellects, Modern Lives*. Chicago: University of Chicago, 1990.

Underhill, Evelyn. *Worship*. New York: Harper and Brothers, 1936.

VanderKam, James C. "Calendars, Ancient Israelite and Early Jewish." Pages 814–20 in vol. 1 of *Anchor Bible Dictionary*. Edited by D. N. Freedman. 6 vols. New York: Doubleday, 1992.

Weisberg, Herbert F., Jon A. Krosnick, and Bruce D. Bowen. *An Introduction to Survey Research, Polling, and Data Analysis*. Thousand Oaks, Calif.: Sage, 1996.

Wiesenberg, Ephraim Jehudah. "Calendar." Pages 43–50 in vol. 5 of *Encyclopedia Judaica*. 16 vols. Jerusalem: Keter, 1978.

Wills, Garry. *Papal Sin: Structures of Deceit*. New York: Doubleday, 2000.

———. "The Tragic Pope?" *New York Review of Books* 41.2 (December 1994): 4–7.

———. "The Vatican Monarchy." *New York Review of Books* 45.3 (February 1998): 20–25.

Woodruff, Paul. "Aristotle on Mimesis." Pages 73–95 in *Essays on Aristotle's Poetics*. Edited by Amélie Oksenberg Rorty. Princeton: Princeton University, 1992.

Index of Names and Subjects

Index of Ancient Sources